True Tales™
of
Howling Winds

Henry Billings
Melissa Stone Billings

STECK-VAUGHN
ELEMENTARY · SECONDARY · ADULT · LIBRARY
A Harcourt Company

www.steck-vaughn.com

Acknowledgments

Editorial Director: Stephanie Muller
Senior Editor: Kristy Schulz
Associate Director of Design: Cynthia Ellis
Design Manager: Alexandra Corona
Production Coordinator: Rebecca Gonzales
Media Researcher: Claudette Landry
Page/Cover Production Artist: Dina Bahan

Cartography: Pp. 4–5, 7, 15, 23, 31, 39, 47, 55, 63, 71, 79, 87, 95, MapQuest.com, Inc.
Illustration Credits: Pp. 13, 21, 37, 45, 53, 69, 77, 85, 93, 101, Eulala Conner
Photo Credits: Cover (background) ©Richard Hamilton Smith/CORBIS; front cover (inset) ©Alan R. Moller/Stone; back cover (inset) ©A&J Verkaik/Skyart; p.6 ©Jim Richardson/CORBIS; pp.8, 9 ©FDR Library; p.10 ©UPI/Corbis–Bettmann; p.14 ©Peter Skinner/Photo Researchers; p.16 ©UPI/Corbis–Bettmann; p.17 ©CORBIS; p.18 ©UPI/Corbis–Bettmann; p.22 ©World Perspectives/Stone; p.24 ©Bleibtreu/SYGMA; p.25 ©Bob Strong/SIPA Press; p.26 ©Bleibtreu/SYGMA; pp.30, 32, 33, 34 ©A&J Verkaik/Skyart; p.38 ©Neil Rabinowitz/Corbis; p.40 ©SYGMA; pp.41, 42 ©Gary Williams/Liaison Agency, Inc.; p.46 ©Peter Lillie;Gallo Images/CORBIS; p.48 ©Wolfgang Kaehler/CORBIS; pp.49, 50 ©AP/Wide World Photos; p.54 ©Charles Doswell III/Stone; p.56 ©SYGMA; p.57a ©AP/Wide World Photos; p.57b ©Wayne Eastep/Stone; p.58 ©Reuters/Adrees A. Latif/Archive Photos; p.62 ©R.W. Jones/CORBIS; pp.64, 65, 66 ©Shimbun/SIPA Press; p.70 ©Science Photo Library/Photo Researchers, inc.; p.72 ©Janez Skok/CORBIS; p.73 ©Hans Georg Roth/CORBIS; p.74 ©Reuters/Savita Kirloskar/Archive Photos; p.78 ©Tony Savino/Sipa Press; p.80 ©AP/Wide World Photos; p.81 ©Kathleen Economou/Allsport; p.82 ©AP/Wide World Photos; p.86 ©Jerry Kobalenko/Stone; p.88 ©AFP/CORBIS; p.89 ©Larry Miller/Science Source/Photo Researchers; p.90 ©Reuters/Peter Andrews/Archive Photos; p.94 ©Ted Soqui/SYGMA; p.96 ©Mark Kraus/SYGMA; p.97 ©Rick Wilking/SYGMA; p.98 ©Lisa Rudy Hoke/Black Star; pp.108a, 108b ©PhotoDisc; p.108c ©Archive Photos; p.108d ©CORBIS; p.109a ©NOAA /Newsmakers/Liaison Agency, Inc.; p.109b ©CORBIS; p.109c ©PhotoDisc.

ISBN 0-7398-2394-9
Copyright © 2001 Steck-Vaughn Company

6 7 8 9 10 11 12 WC 10 09 08 07 06 05

Contents

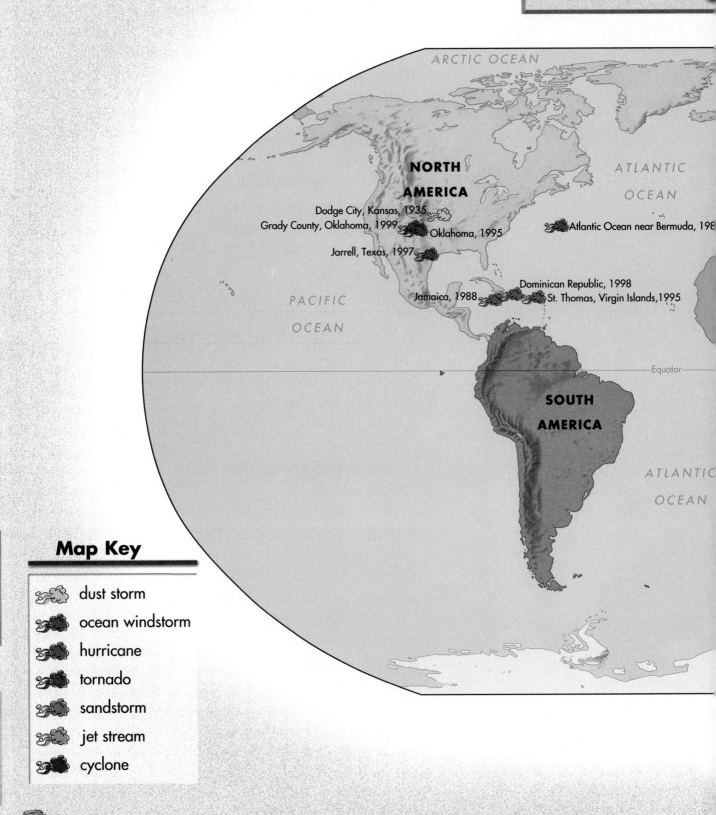

ARCTIC OCEAN

NORTH AMERICA

Dodge City, Kansas, 1935
Grady County, Oklahoma, 1999
Oklahoma, 1995

ATLANTIC OCEAN

Atlantic Ocean near Bermuda, 198

Jarrell, Texas, 1997

PACIFIC OCEAN

Dominican Republic, 1998
Jamaica, 1988   St. Thomas, Virgin Islands, 1995

Equator

SOUTH AMERICA

ATLANTIC OCEAN

Map Key

- dust storm
- ocean windstorm
- hurricane
- tornado
- sandstorm
- jet stream
- cyclone

ARCTIC OCEAN

EUROPE

ASIA

Sea of

Air over Pacific Ocean near Tokyo, Japan, 1997

Egypt, 1997

Kandla, India, 1998

PACIFIC

OCEAN

AFRICA

INDIAN

OCEAN

AUSTRALIA

Umtata, South Africa, 1998

N
W   E
S

ANTARCTICA

Dust, Dust, and More Dust

The people of Kansas were tired of dust. For weeks, clouds of dust had blown through Kansas. The dust was thick and **dense**. The people tried to stay out of it as much as possible. Then on April 14, 1935, the dust seemed to be less. In fact, on this day, the air seemed fresh and clear. The sun was shining. At last, people could go outside. Many people began planting gardens. Others hung clothes on the line. Some even packed up a lunch for a Sunday picnic. Although the day started off nicely, it wasn't going to stay that way.

A Black Cloud

Thirteen-year-old Harley Holladay lived on a farm near Dodge City, Kansas. Like everyone else, he was excited by the clear, sunny day. He wanted to be out enjoying the good weather. So that morning, Harley decided to walk to a nearby pond to skip stones. His mother stayed home to clean. Mrs. Holladay carried chairs out onto the lawn. She cleaned off all the dust that had built up on them. She also brought rugs outside and began to beat the dust out of them.

Not far away, 15-year-old Opal Musselman went out with her family. They decided to take a drive to visit a friend. It was nice to be out without worrying about the dust.

As the morning went on, the **temperature** rose. Soon it was almost 90 **degrees**. But no one minded the heat. Everyone was just glad the day was clear.

That afternoon, however, the fine day quickly came to an end. Shortly after lunch, the temperature began to drop. It fell 50 degrees in just a few hours.

The cloud of dust looked as if it was rolling over the land.

Birds began chirping wildly. They seemed to sense that something was wrong. Then, around 2:40 P.M., a black cloud appeared in the distance.

The black cloud was not high in the air. It was right on the ground. People who saw it knew that a **dust storm** was on the way. Wind had picked up loose dirt off the ground. The wind was blowing this dirt through the air. The cloud of dirt that formed was called a "roller." That's because it looked as if it was rolling over the land.

Dust Storms

Kansas had seen plenty of dust storms in the past few years. One reason for this was lack of rain. A **drought** had turned the ground dry and dusty. The problem was made even worse because farmers had plowed up too much land to grow crops. They had plowed up the land hoping that rain would come and make the land **moist**. But the rain did not come, and the plowed land just sat there full of loosened dirt. As soon as a strong wind came along, this dirt was swept up into the air.

The dust storm that blew up this day was the worst yet. In fact, people called it a "Black **Blizzard**." By that, they meant that the wind seemed as strong as the wind in a snowy blizzard. But in this blizzard of dust, the air was not white. It was black. April 14th became known as "Black Sunday."

Dust and Dirt Everywhere

Harley Holladay was still at the pond when he saw the dust storm coming. The cloud of dust was more than a mile high. Holladay rushed home to warn his family. He helped his mother gather up all the chairs and rugs. By then, the sky was very black. The wind was blowing **fiercely**. Dust and dirt were **swirling** everywhere. Holladay couldn't see more than a few feet in front of him. He had to crawl on his hands and knees to get back to the house.

Opal Musselman and her family saw the cloud coming, too. They hoped to drive home before it reached them. But the dust storm swept over their car. Musselman's uncle was driving when the storm hit. He couldn't see the road. Musselman stuck her

The dust storm swept over roads and fields.

It was very hard to see and walk in the dust storm.

head out the window to help tell him where to drive. The dust flew into her face. It burned her nose and made her eyes water. The Musselmans were only seven miles from their house. Still, it took them over two hours to get home.

Other drivers left their cars by the road. They tried to run through the storm. Some got lost. Still, others grabbed onto wire fences. They used the fence wires to feel their way along until they came to a house or barn.

Even people indoors were frightened by the storm. Lila Lee King was eleven years old at the time. "I was sure I was going to die," said King. "We lit matches and held them before our face. We couldn't see the light unless it was quite close."

Kansas was not the only state hit by the dust storm. Parts of Oklahoma, Texas, New Mexico, and Colorado were hit, too. Fences, sheds, and tractors were buried in the dust. Many farm animals died.

The next day, a newspaper writer named this **region** the "Dust Bowl." Over the next five years, other dust storms came. Only in 1940 did the drought end. Then the awful years of the "Dust Bowl" were finally over.

Read and Remember — Choose the Answer

Draw a circle around the correct answer.

1. Why did Mrs. Holladay bring rugs outside?

to sell them   to clean them   to sew them

2. What did the birds begin to do shortly after lunch?

make nests   eat seeds   chirp wildly

3. What was the huge cloud of dirt called?

dirt ball   snow dust   roller

4. How did Harley Holladay get back to the house?

by crawling   by running   by sliding

5. What did a newspaper writer call the states hit by dust?

the Black Land   the Dust Bowl   the Dry Fields

Write About It

Imagine you are Harley Holladay or Opal Musselman. Write a short paragraph telling how you felt as the dust storm arrived.

_____

_____

_____

_____

_____

_____

Focus on Vocabulary — Find the Meaning

Read each sentence. Circle the best meaning for the word in dark print.

1. The dust was **dense**.

   light   thick   black

2. As the morning went on, the **temperature** rose.

   water   measure of heat   fear

3. Soon it was 90 **degrees**.

   units for measuring heat   time units   weight units

4. A **dust storm** was coming.

   wind that blows dust   wind and rain   thunder

5. A **drought** killed the crops.

   lack of rain   storm cloud   thunder

6. The ground was not **moist**.

   dusty   grassy   a bit wet

7. People called it a black **blizzard**.

   heavy snowstorm   sand pile   machine

8. The wind blew **fiercely**.

   strongly   loudly   quietly

9. The **swirling** cloud scared Lila Lee King.

   floating   sitting   spinning

10. Storms hurt the whole **region**.

    road   area of land   town

Causes of the Dust Bowl

During the Dust Bowl, strong winds were able to blow soil and dust easily into the air. The diagram below shows some causes of the Dust Bowl. Study the diagram. Circle the answer that best completes each sentence.

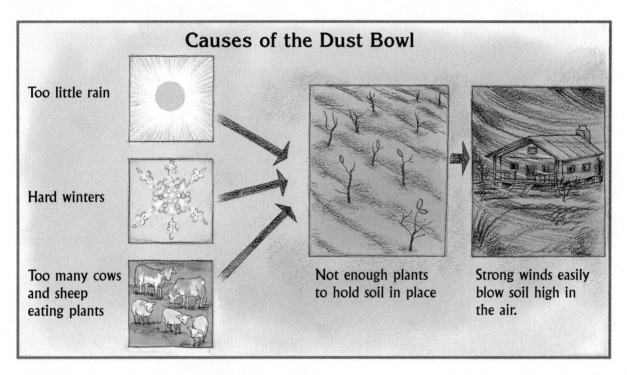

Causes of the Dust Bowl

Too little rain

Hard winters

Too many cows and sheep eating plants

Not enough plants to hold soil in place

Strong winds easily blow soil high in the air.

1. One cause of the Dust Bowl was _____.
   easy winters   too many plants   too little rain

2. Cows helped cause the Dust Bowl because they _____.
   ate plants   made the soil flat   drank the water

3. Plants were important because they _____.
   needed water   held soil in place   blocked the sun

4. Strong winds blew _____ high into the air.
   soil   water   rain

Tall Ship in Trouble

On June 2, 1984, the *Marques* set sail from Bermuda. Forty-one other ships also left this island in the Atlantic Ocean. The ships were in an 800-mile race. They were on their way to Nova Scotia, Canada.

It was a race rule that half of each ship's crew had to be between 16 and 25 years old. The race was supposed to teach these young people about sailing on the open sea. But the sea can be a dangerous place. The crew of the *Marques* was about to find that out.

High Winds

Like the other ships in the race, the *Marques* was a "tall ship." It had huge sails. It was also very long, measuring 117 feet. For this race, the *Marques* carried 28 people. That included Captain Stuart Finlay, his wife, and their one-year-old son. It also included seven full-time sailors. The rest of the crew was made up of young people. For some, it was their first time ever on a big ship.

Before leaving Bermuda, the racers checked the weather. Strong winds were expected in the Atlantic Ocean. These winds were supposed to blow as strong as 38 miles per hour.

That did not worry race **officials**. They felt the tall ships would be able to handle such winds. They saw no reason to put off the race. "We would not have sent the **fleet** if there had been any question of bad weather," said race official Oliver Pemberton. "Some of those sailing had never put out to sea. We would not want to put them at **risk**."

So that afternoon, the ships took off as planned. In the middle of the night, the wind did pick up. There were **gusts** of 40 and even 45 miles per hour. The sea turned rough. The young sailors on the *Marques* worked hard to keep the ship steady.

No One Saw It Coming

By 4 A.M. on June 3, the storm had died down. It looked like the worst was over. "The skies cleared," recalled 24-year-old William Barnhardt. "It was calm and we could see the stars."

But suddenly, the *Marques* ran into a **squall**. This was a small but very strong storm. It carried rain and high winds. No one on the ship saw the squall coming. But the squall whipped toward the *Marques* at about 65 miles per hour.

Most of the sailors on the ship were asleep when the squall struck. They were in their cabins below deck. Twenty-two-year-old Philip Sefton was steering the ship. He had sailed the ship through many bad

No one on the *Marques* expected a squall to hit.

The squall was a sudden, strong storm that caused large waves.

windstorms. "But I could not believe this storm," he later said.

Sefton shouted to the sailors below deck. He quickly ordered them to leave their cabins and come up to the deck. But even as he gave this order, a **tremendous** gust of wind hit the *Marques*. It knocked the ship over onto its side. Then a large wave washed over the ship's deck. Sefton tried twice to steer the ship but it was no use. The raging water was too strong. In less than one minute, the tall ship sank beneath the waves.

Sefton was swept over the side of the sinking ship. He swam free of the *Marques* as it went down. But those who were still in their beds never stood a chance. The Finlays, along with 16 others, drowned.

A Lucky Few

Andrew Freeman, age 22, was one of the lucky ones. His **shift** had ended at 4 A.M. He should have been in bed. But he stayed up on deck to enjoy the early morning. Freeman later said, "The boat was sailing along really well and fast. It was a nice feeling to be up there." When the ship suddenly tipped over, he managed to swim away.

Clifton McMillan was also very lucky. He, too, had just finished his shift. The 16-year-old McMillan went below deck. But he didn't go to bed. Instead, he followed the ship's rules and waited at the bottom of the stairs in case he was needed to help change the sails. That's where he was when the ship tipped over.

"Water started pouring in," McMillan said. He fought his way through the water up to the deck. "Five of us below **struggled** to get out," he said. "When I next looked, only three of us made it." McMillan and the others were quickly swept out into the water. As the *Marques* sank, McMillan saw a **life raft** in front of him. He jumped onto it and then he reached out and pulled the others on board.

In all, nine people made it off the *Marques*. Somehow, they all reached life rafts. By then, the deadly wind was already dying down. It went away as quickly as it came. A few hours later, the nine people in life rafts were picked up by another tall ship.

John Ash was one of the nine who lived. He was later asked about the wind that had sunk the ship. The 24-year-old described it in five short words. He said, "It meant to kill us."

Captain Finlay's wife and son were two of the 19 people who had drowned.

Read and Remember — Check the Events

Place a check in front of the three sentences that tell what happened in the story.

_____ **1.** Stuart Finlay refused to sail on the *Marques*.

_____ **2.** Most of the people on the *Marques* were below deck when the squall hit.

_____ **3.** The *Marques* tipped over and sank quickly.

_____ **4.** Philip Sefton died when he jumped off the ship.

_____ **5.** Only nine people that were on the *Marques* lived through the storm.

_____ **6.** The captain of the ship forgot to warn his crew.

Think About It — Cause and Effect

A **cause** is something that makes something else happen. What happens is called the **effect**. Match each cause with an effect. Write the letter on the correct blank. The first one is done for you.

Cause	Effect
1. Andrew Freeman wanted to enjoy the morning, so __**b**__	**a.** the people below deck had no time to escape.
2. Clifton McMillan knew he might need to help change the sails, so _____	**b.** he stayed up on deck.
3. Officials felt the ships could take the winds, so _____	**c.** they decided not to stop the race.
4. The ship sank very quickly, so _____	**d.** the people on the *Marques* thought the worst was over.
5. The first storm ended, so _____	**e.** he waited at the bottom of the stairs.

Focus on Vocabulary — Match Up

Match each word with its meaning. Darken the circle beside the correct answer.

1. officials

○ people in charge   ○ sailors   ○ teachers

2. fleet

○ captains   ○ crew members   ○ group of ships

3. risk

○ dark   ○ danger   ○ last place

4. gusts

○ sails   ○ strong bursts of wind   ○ high waves

5. squall

○ small but strong storm   ○ scream   ○ island

6. windstorms

○ storms with strong winds   ○ waves   ○ race rules

7. tremendous

○ little   ○ very big   ○ scary

8. shift

○ work period   ○ boat   ○ sail

9. struggled

○ forgot   ○ swam quickly   ○ worked hard

10. life raft

○ jacket   ○ small boat   ○ mask

Wind Direction

The four main directions are north (N), south (S), east (E), and west (W). A **wind vane** shows the direction from which a wind blows. The vane points into the wind. A west wind blows from the west, so the wind vane would point west. Study the diagrams. Write the answer to each question.

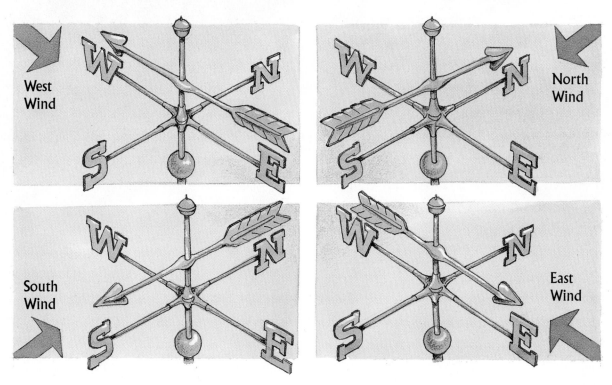

1. What does a wind vane show? _____

    _____

2. If a wind vane points south (S), what kind of wind is blowing?

    _____

3. If a wind vane points north (N), from which direction is the wind

    coming? _____

4. If an east wind is blowing, where does a wind vane point? _____

5. Does a wind vane tell how fast a wind is blowing? _____

High Winds Blast Jamaica

The warning came on September 11, 1988. A **hurricane** was headed toward the Caribbean island of Jamaica. The storm would bring plenty of rain. It would also bring very high winds.

Jamaicans were used to hurricane warnings. Between the months of June and November, such storms often swept past their island. But the hurricane that hit on the twelfth of September was the worst **natural disaster** ever to hit Jamaica.

A Strong Storm

Like many hurricanes, this one began as a tiny storm off the **coast** of Africa. It moved west over a warm part of the Atlantic Ocean. Along the way, it picked up moist air. This air rose up over the ocean to form thick, spinning clouds. Slowly, the small storm grew stronger. On September 10, it became a hurricane. It was given the name Hurricane Gilbert.

All hurricanes are **rated** by their wind speeds. They are placed into a **category**. A category 1 hurricane is the weakest. Its winds are between 74 and 95 miles per hour. A category 5 hurricane is the strongest. It has winds over 155 miles per hour. Hurricane Gilbert was a category 5 storm. Near the ground, its winds reached 175 miles per hour. But up in the air, Hurricane Gilbert's winds were moving at about 200 miles per hour!

After crossing the Atlantic Ocean, Hurricane Gilbert reached the Caribbean Sea. It brushed by Puerto Rico and Haiti without causing too much

Hurricane Gilbert's strong winds caused a lot of damage.

damage. Then it headed straight for Jamaica. By noon on September 12, 1988, it neared the Jamaican city of Kingston. The sky grew dark. Heavy rain began to fall. High winds blew in.

These winds were worse than anything Jamaicans had ever seen before. The winds smashed windows. They tipped over airplanes and ripped whole trees right out of the ground. They knocked down power lines. Before long, Jamaica had no **electricity**. "There was no power, no water, no phones, no radio, nothing," said one man. "The place was wrecked."

Scary Times

The high winds blew the roofs off eight out of every ten houses in Jamaica. Alphonso Tyrell was with his wife and seven children when Hurricane Gilbert hit. They lay **nervously** on the floor in their home. Then Tyrell saw his thin metal roof beginning to lift off in the wind. He jumped up and grabbed at it, trying to keep it from blowing away. But it was no use. "Another puff came and licked it away from me," he said. "The children started crying. My wife started crying. Then the whole room got blown away, all the walls gone." Luckily, Tyrell and his family were not hurt.

Mertylin Anderson and her family were almost killed by the fierce winds. Anderson was with her husband and two young sons. They were waiting out the hurricane in their one-room house. The strong winds pulled a tree out of the ground and carried it through the air. The winds drove the tree right into the house. The Andersons were not badly hurt, but their home was smashed to pieces.

The hurricane also damaged big buildings. One bank in Jamaica had its walls smashed. The wind picked up checks from inside the bank and blew them all over the city. "There were checks blowing around everywhere," said Jackie Stewart, a visitor to the island.

Hospitals lost their roofs. Some also had parts of their walls blown away. Like most people, doctors had no electricity. They had to do their work without light. All they had were a few flashlights.

As night fell, the wind and rain continued. Sylvia Dyer was in one of the hospitals that was hit hard by the hurricane. "It was **terrifying**," she said. "You hear

The hurricane ripped whole trees right out of the ground.

the glass breaking and things falling down. In the day you can see things, but at night you only hear the sound."

Building a New Jamaica

At last, Hurricane Gilbert left Jamaica. But by then, the country was in bad shape. The storm had killed 45 people. It left 500,000 others without homes. It also wiped out almost all of the country's crops. Many Jamaicans earned money by growing fruit, coconuts, and coffee. Without these crops, people had no way to earn a living. "We have to build a completely new Jamaica," said one woman.

It would not be easy. But Jamaicans had been through hard times before. They worked hard to put their country back together again. Some people had said it would take Jamaica ten years to get over the storm. But after just one year, the island was doing well again. Homes had been rebuilt. Crops had been replanted. Beaches, roads, and **hillsides** had been cleaned up. Jamaica was once again a place where people could enjoy sun, sand, and good times.

Hurricane Gilbert left 500,000 people without homes.

Read and Remember — Finish the Sentence

Circle the best ending for each sentence.

1. The people of Jamaica were used to _____.
   heavy snow   hurricane warnings   cool summers

2. Hurricane Gilbert moved across the _____.
   state of Florida   Atlantic Ocean   island of Cuba

3. Because of its wind speed, Hurricane Gilbert was placed in category _____.
   one   five   ten

4. The storm winds caused most houses in Jamaica to _____.
   burn down   lose their roofs   wash away

5. Doctors had to work without _____.
   masks   coats   electricity

Write About It

Imagine you have just lived through Hurricane Gilbert. Write a short letter to a friend, describing how you feel.

Dear _____,

_____

_____

_____

_____

_____

Focus on Vocabulary — Finish the Paragraphs

Use the words in dark print to complete the paragraphs. Reread the paragraphs to be sure they make sense.

damage	**electricity**	**coast**	**hurricane**
rated	**category**	**terrifying**	**nervously**
hillsides	**natural disaster**		

In September 1988, a tiny storm began over the ocean waters off the **(1)**_____ of Africa. As it moved west, it became stronger and stronger. The windy storm grew into a very powerful **(2)**_____. It was **(3)**_____ by its wind speed. With winds over 175 miles per hour, it was placed in the highest **(4)**_____.

The storm was the worst event or **(5)**_____ ever to hit Jamaica. It knocked out **(6)**_____ all over the island. People thought the storm was **(7)**_____. Roofs of houses were blown away. The people of Jamaica waited **(8)**_____ for the strong winds and rain to pass.

Finally, the storm ended. Then the people saw how much **(9)**_____ it had done. The storm had ruined many houses and buildings. It took the people of Jamaica more than one year to clean up the beaches, roads, and **(10)**_____.

Effects of Hurricanes

Some **hurricanes** are much stronger than others. Scientists place a hurricane into a **category** based on its wind speed. The chart below compares the speeds and effects of different hurricanes. Study the chart. Circle the answer to each question.

Hurricane Categories

Category	Wind Speeds (in miles per hour)	Effects
1	74–95	Damages trees, bushes, weak homes, and signs.
2	96–110	Blows small trees down. Damages some roofs and weak homes. Causes some flooding.
3	111–130	Blows many large trees down. Causes flooding. Damages some roofs, windows, and stronger buildings.
4	131–155	Blows trees and all signs down. Damages most roofs and windows. Tears apart weak homes. Causes much flooding.
5	More than 155	Blows trees and all signs down. Tears apart many buildings. Causes great flooding.

1. How many categories for hurricanes are there?

3   5   7

2. What is used to place a hurricane in a category?

amount of rain   effect on rivers   wind speed

3. In which category is a hurricane with a wind speed of 150 miles per hour?

category 4   category 3   category 2

4. What can a category 3 hurricane damage?

strong buildings   all signs   only roofs

5. Which hurricane can cause great flooding?

category 1   category 2   category 5

Chasing the Wind

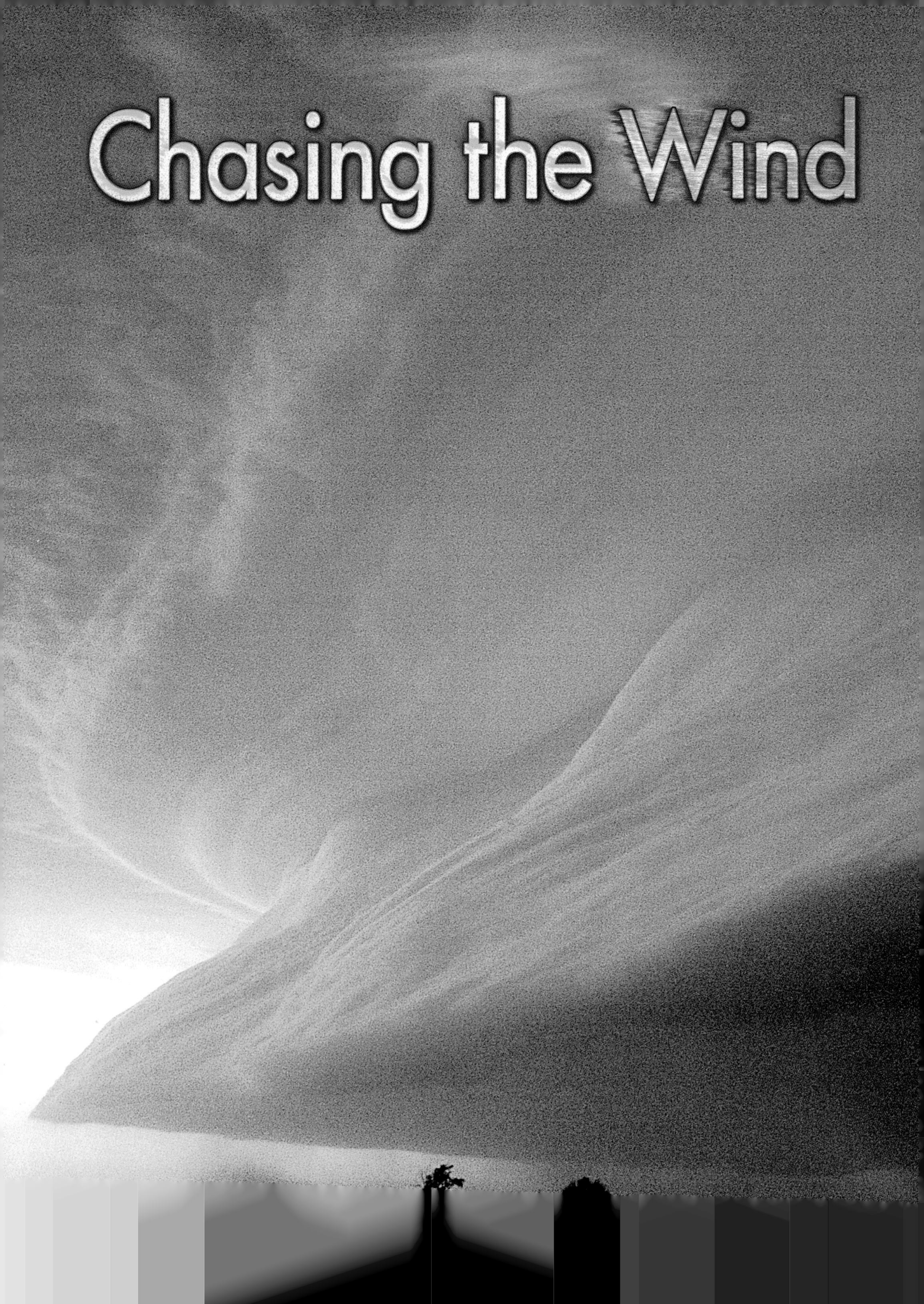

Ed and Jerrine Verkaik were in a hurry. They were following a **thunderstorm** as it moved across Oklahoma. Jerrine was driving. Her husband Ed was looking out the window. The Verkaiks loved to study different types of weather. They studied everything from rainbows to sky color. But they especially loved to study **tornadoes**. In June 1995, they were hoping a tornado would form from the black clouds they had spotted.

Dangerous Storms

Tornadoes are small but powerful windstorms. Tornadoes are sometimes called **twisters**. That's because the wind spins around in a tight **spiral**. From far away, a tornado can look like a long twisted rope that reaches from the clouds down to the ground.

Most people try to stay away from tornadoes. But the Verkaiks were tornado **chasers**. They followed tornadoes every chance they got. They tried to get close enough to take pictures of the tornadoes. They also wrote down notes. There was a lot that **scientists** did not understand about tornadoes. The Verkaiks were hoping their notes and pictures would help scientists learn more about these powerful and sometimes deadly windstorms. The Verkaiks hoped that someday scientists could do a better job of warning people about tornadoes before they hit. An **accurate** warning about when and where tornadoes might hit could help save many lives.

Ed and Jerrine Verkaik love to study tornadoes.

To find tornadoes, Ed and Jerrine Verkaik followed thunderstorms. It is during some of these storms that tornadoes can form. In a thunderstorm, cold, dry air runs into warm, wet air. If there is a big difference in temperature, a strong wind begins to blow. This wind can begin to swirl in a tight circle. Then it can drop down out of the sky. When this swirling wind comes near the ground, it is called a tornado.

Tornadoes are not very wide. They are usually less than a mile across. Some are not much wider than a basketball court. Tornadoes don't last long, either. Often, they travel about a mile before winding down.

Still, tornadoes can form in just a few minutes. They move with the storm cloud they are part of. Because tornadoes are usually not very large, it is hard to know when and where they will hit. Tornadoes are also very strong. They can **destroy** everything in their path. Some tornadoes are even stronger than hurricanes. A strong hurricane might have winds that blow at about 150 miles per hour. But a really strong tornado can have winds that blow at more than 300 miles per hour!

Like hurricanes, tornadoes are rated by wind speed. A man named Ted Fujita came up with the Fujita **scale**, or F-scale for short. This scale is used to measure the wind speed in tornadoes. On this scale, the strongest tornadoes are rated F-5. They have wind speeds greater than 261 miles per hour. A wind this strong can send cars flying hundreds of feet through the air. It can rip bark off trees. It can even pick up a house and carry it away.

Knowing Where to Look

The Verkaiks had been chasing tornadoes for years. Every April they left their home in Ontario, Canada. They climbed into their car and drove down into Tornado Alley. This is a stretch of land that runs from north Texas to south Iowa. It is where most tornadoes occur in the United States. From April to June, the air in the Tornado Alley is often just right for tornadoes to form.

While many storm chasers travel in fancy vans, the Verkaiks used a car. Jerrine did all the driving. Ed couldn't drive. He lost one leg and much of his sight

The Verkaiks took this photo of a tornado they chased.

The tornado spun out of the clouds and touched the ground.

in a lab **accident** when he was younger. Still, he saw shapes in the sky. Beyond that, he often had a feeling for when and where tornadoes might show up.

A Close Call

Even with Ed and Jerrine's understanding of tornadoes, there was still a lot of guessing involved. In the 30 years that the Verkaiks had been chasing these swirling windstorms, they had spotted only about 40 tornadoes. They had gotten close enough to take pictures of about half of them.

In June 1995, the Verkaiks guessed just right. A tornado spun down out of the clouds. But it started moving right toward their car. Suddenly, Ed and Jerrine were in danger of being killed.

"The tornado was just 20 yards ahead," said Jerrine. "I couldn't back up. There were cars behind us." So she decided to do the only thing she could. "I just whipped around and drove the wrong way down the highway." Luckily, the Verkaiks got away safely. But this close call did not stop them. The Verkaiks kept chasing tornadoes.

Read and Remember — Choose the Answer

Draw a circle around the correct answer.

1. What do tornadoes often look like?
   a high wall   a spinning ball   a long, twisted rope

2. What did the Verkaiks do when they got near tornadoes?
   took pictures   stood still   sat down

3. How are tornadoes rated?
   by wind speed   by height   by distance

4. Where did the Verkaiks look for tornadoes?
   on Twister Hill   in Tornado Alley   in Storm Valley

5. How far do most tornadoes travel before winding down?
   a mile   a hundred miles   a thousand miles

6. How close did a tornado get to the Verkaik's car in June 1995?
   20 yards   3 feet   1 mile

Think About It — Find the Main Ideas

Underline the two most important ideas from the story.

1. Ed Verkaik lost a leg and much of his sight in a lab accident.
2. The Verkaiks chased tornadoes to gather information about these powerful storms.
3. In June 1995, the Verkaiks came dangerously close to a tornado.
4. Ed and Jerrine Verkaik lived in Ontario, Canada.
5. The Verkaiks sometimes studied rainbows and sky color.
6. A man named Ted Fujita came up with a way of rating tornadoes.

Focus on Vocabulary — Crossword Puzzle

Use the clues to complete the puzzle. Choose from the words in dark print.

accurate   spiral   thunderstorm   destroy   accident

tornadoes   chasers   scientists   scale   twisters

Across

3. storm with thunder and lightning

5. people who follow something

6. ruin or tear apart

8. people who study science

9. exactly right

Down

1. powerful storms with strong, spinning winds

2. a harmful event that is not expected

3. another name for tornadoes

4. standard of measurement

7. a curve that winds around

How a Tornado Begins

A **tornado** begins when warm, rising air starts to spin inside a **thundercloud**. The air begins to spin in a tube, which sends a long **funnel** toward the ground. Study the tornado diagram below. Write the answer to each question.

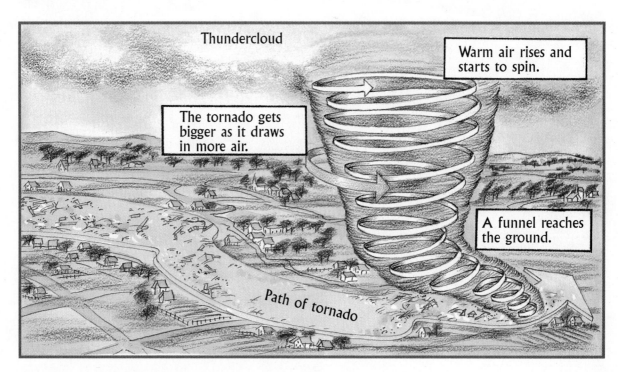

Thundercloud

Warm air rises and starts to spin.

The tornado gets bigger as it draws in more air.

A funnel reaches the ground.

Path of tornado

1. In what kind of cloud can a tornado form? _____

2. What rises and starts to spin? _____

3. What part of a tornado reaches the ground? _____

4. What is the area of ground where a tornado moves called? _____

_____

5. How does a tornado get bigger? _____

September Surprise

Joyce and George Thomas thought they were ready for Hurricane Marilyn. They had plenty of water and food in the house. They also had their flashlight handy.

The Thomases live on St. Thomas, an island in the Caribbean Sea. St. Thomas is part of the Virgin Islands. Hurricanes often sweep through this area. So people knew what to do when a storm approached on September 15, 1995. But as Joyce Thomas later said, "No matter how much you try to prepare for a hurricane, it is never quite enough."

No Big Thing

As Hurricane Marilyn made its way toward St. Thomas, scientists watched the storm closely. They measured its wind speed. Then they rated it. Hurricane categories are numbered 1 to 5. A category 1 is the weakest kind of hurricane. A category 5 is the strongest. Scientists rated the winds of Hurricane Marilyn a category 2 hurricane. That meant the winds were between 96 and 110 miles per hour.

To the people of St. Thomas, that didn't sound too bad. In fact, many people called it a "little" hurricane. Three other hurricanes had passed by the island in the past four weeks. One had been rated a category 4, meaning it had winds of up to 155 miles per hour. So as one woman said, Hurricane Marilyn sounded like "no big thing."

But Hurricane Marilyn was about to surprise people. As the storm moved along, it gained speed. Its wind rose to 115 miles per hour. It moved from a category 2 hurricane to a category 3 hurricane.

In addition, this storm took a different path from the ones before it. The others had not come very close to St. Thomas. But Hurricane Marilyn headed right for it.

As night came, the rain grew heavy. By 8 P.M., the wind was blowing so hard that it sounded like it was roaring. Joyce Thomas heard it whistling through her sliding glass doors. She and her husband decided it was time to move into the bathroom. That was the safest room in the house. It had no windows. So if the wind **shattered** any glass, the Thomases wouldn't be cut.

Elsewhere on the island, others also tried to prepare for the rising wind. Matthew Yarde and his father nailed boards across the doorway of their home. They hoped the boards would help keep the wind and rain out. Even in the island's fancy hotels, people began to get nervous. Many people did what Matthew and Kimberly Benne did. They **huddled** in the bathroom and hoped for the best.

This photo from space shows the spinning clouds of Hurricane Marilyn.

The strong winds of the hurricane tossed airplanes around at the airport.

Broken Glass and Flying Roofs

As the hours passed, the full **force** of Hurricane Marilyn hit St. Thomas. Leaves were pulled off the trees. Telephone poles were ripped out of the ground. A sailboat was carried through the air and dumped into a swimming pool. The wind even tossed around airplanes parked at the airport.

Everywhere, windows and glass doors were blown out. Joyce Thomas's sliding glass doors shattered. So did the glass door leading out of the Bennes' hotel room. The Yardes had no glass in their door. The wind blew off the wooden boards they had nailed across the doorway.

For the Thomases, the worst was yet to come. They began to hear a creaking sound. Looking up, they realized that the metal roof was being **pried** loose by the wind. "Suddenly, water **gushed** down on us," Joyce later wrote. "Pointing the flashlight upward, we saw that there was nothing over our head but the swirling **elements**."

The Thomases quickly moved into a closet at the other end of the house. They thought they would be safer there. That part of the roof had not blown off. For the next few hours, they waited in the closet for the storm to end.

An Island in Bad Shape

At one point, the wind did die down. That was when the **eye** of the hurricane passed over the island. In the very center of the storm, the air was calm. But the quiet didn't last long. Within minutes, the powerful wind returned. Once again, tremendous gusts shook the island.

By morning, Hurricane Marilyn had moved past St. Thomas. But by then, the island was in **shambles**. Joyce Thomas couldn't believe what the storm had done to her house. The strong wind had blown away everything but the walls. "Even our furniture was gone," said Joyce. "It looked as though someone had moved us out."

Matthew Yarde also was **shocked**. When he walked outside, he saw house after house with its roof blown off. Nearly every building on St. Thomas had been damaged. Six people had died in the terrible storm. Those who **survived** had a lot of cleaning up to do. None of them would ever again think of Marilyn as a "little" hurricane.

People on St. Thomas would never again think of Marilyn as a little hurricane.

Read and Remember — Check the Events

Place a check in front of the three sentences that tell what happened in the story.

_____ **1.** Hurricane Marilyn was a category 1 hurricane.

_____ **2.** Joyce and George Thomas tried to prepare for Hurricane Marilyn.

_____ **3.** The Bennes left St. Thomas just in time.

_____ **4.** The storm blew the roof off Joyce Thomas's home.

_____ **5.** Hurricane Marilyn was the first hurricane to pass through the Caribbean in twelve years.

_____ **6.** Nearly every building in St. Thomas was damaged.

Write About It

Imagine you have moved to St. Thomas. Write a paragraph describing what you would do if a hurricane headed toward the island.

_____

_____

_____

_____

_____

_____

_____

_____

_____

Focus on Vocabulary — Finish Up

Choose the correct word in dark print to complete each sentence.

force	**pried**	**shattered**	**elements**
shocked	**survived**	**eye**	**gushed**
huddled	**shambles**		

1. The center of a hurricane is the _____.

2. To have lived through something is to have _____.

3. To be suddenly surprised and upset is to be _____.

4. Glass that has broken into many pieces has _____.

5. Rain, wind, and snow are different kinds of weather _____.

6. The strength and power of a storm is its _____.

7. To have _____ means to have gathered closely together.

8. Something that has been pulled loose with great strength has been _____ loose.

9. If something is a mess, it is in _____.

10. Water that flowed very quickly is water that _____.

A Look at a Hurricane

A **hurricane** begins as a small **thunderstorm** over a warm ocean. First, warm air rises and cooler air moves in. Then the air in the storm starts to spin. The storm grows larger and stronger, with huge clouds and spinning winds. Study the diagram. Write the answer to each question.

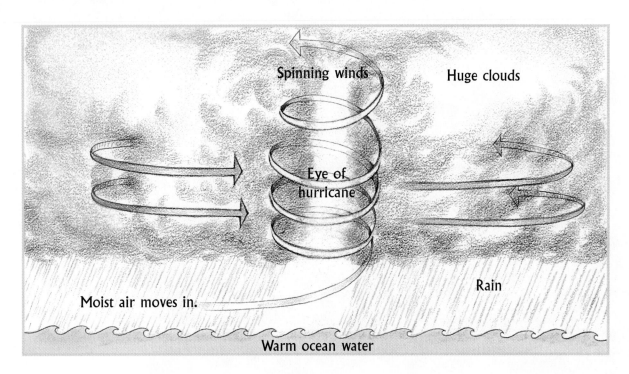

Spinning winds

Huge clouds

Eye of hurricane

Rain

Moist air moves in.

Warm ocean water

1. What is the center of a hurricane called? _____

2. Does warm air or cool air rise? _____

3. Over what kind of water does a hurricane begin? _____

4. What falls from the clouds? _____

5. Do the winds move in a straight line? _____

6. Is there rain in the eye of the hurricane? _____

Sandstorm!

Ten-year-old Mohammed Selim lived in Egypt. Like everyone else in this northern African country, he knew that spring can be a dangerous time. For about 50 days each spring, strong wind blows across Egypt. This wind often carries sand from nearby **deserts**. The sand fills the air, making it hard to see and to breathe.

Selim had been in several **sandstorms**. But he was not prepared for the one that hit on May 2, 1997. That sandstorm was the worst to blow across Egypt in more than 30 years.

Turning Day into Night

The storm began far to the west. There, wind blew over the Sahara Desert and Libyan Desert. It picked up **ton** after ton of loose sand from the desert floor. The wind carried this sand east along the north coast of Africa. As it moved, the storm gained strength. Its wind blew about 60 miles an hour.

The sandstorm reached Egypt just after 3 P.M. As it approached, the sky went from blue to gray. From a distance, the blowing sand seemed to glow red. But as it came nearer, the whole sky turned white. There was so much sand in the air that no one could see a thing. **Visibility** was zero. The dense cloud of sand moved across the land.

Within seconds, the sand blocked out the sun. Cities and towns suddenly grew dark. One man said the storm "turned day into night."

Mohammed Selim was riding his donkey when the storm hit. He and the animal were both knocked down by the fierce wind. Blowing sand began to

The strong winds picked up loose sand from nearby deserts.

wash over them. Soon Selim and the donkey were buried under the hot, dry sand.

Other Egyptians were caught outside, too. They could not believe what was happening around them. Most sandstorms were just a **nuisance**. But this storm was different. The blowing sand was strong enough to kill people.

As the storm struck, some people thought the world was coming to an end. They screamed and shouted. They ran blindly through the streets. The sand and dust made it almost impossible to breathe. So people coughed and choked as they felt their way through the streets. Those in cars could not see where they were going. One small bus tumbled into the Nile River. Another hit a car and a bicycle.

The Bad Wind

The wind was so strong that it **threatened** to pick people right up off the ground. So some people wrapped their arms around lampposts. Others grabbed telephone poles. They held onto anything that was **anchored** down.

Debris flew through the air. People were hit by broken tree branches that were blown by the wind. Many others were cut by pieces of flying glass. Some people were hurt when large signs blew over and landed on them.

Some of the flying debris killed people. Ragab Ali died after a palm tree flew through the air and landed on him. Another man was killed by part of a satellite dish. The wind ripped the heavy metal dish out of the ground. The dish spun wildly through the air. As it did so, it hit and killed the man.

Other people were killed by things they thought would keep them safe. Three people ducked under the **balcony** of a house. They thought the house would keep them out of the wind. But the wind blew the house apart. The roof and walls caved in. All three people under the balcony were crushed.

Another woman looked for safety under a tree. But the wind **uprooted** the tree. With its roots above ground, the tree tipped over and killed the woman underneath it.

Sadly, Mohammed Selim also died in the storm. As the wind stopped blowing, people hurried to dig the

People had trouble walking in the strong winds of the sandstorm.

boy and his donkey out of the sand. The high winds had only lasted about 20 minutes. So people thought that Selim might still be alive. But when the people dug him out and brushed away the sand, they saw that they were too late to save him.

Sand Problems

Selim was one of the 24 people that died in the storm. Many more were hurt. Luckily, the storm hit on a Friday. That is a day of the week when most Egyptians don't work. So many people were at home. The streets were not as crowded as they would have been otherwise.

Even after the sandstorm died down, problems remained. Small bits of sand and dust still hung in the air. Also, the wind had blown many bugs in from the desert. One doctor warned parents to put masks on small children before taking them outside. It would be many days before the air in Egypt would return to normal. The memories of the sandstorm would last much longer than that.

Even after the sandstorm, the sand in the air made it hard to breathe.

Read and Remember — Finish the Sentence

Circle the best ending for each sentence.

1. Mohammed Selim lived in _____.
   Israel   Libya   Egypt

2. Strong wind blows across Egypt in the _____.
   spring   summer   fall

3. When the storm hit, Mohammed Selim was riding his _____.
   horse   bicycle   donkey

4. Many people were cut by pieces of _____.
   sharp wire   flying glass   paper

5. The high winds lasted about _____.
   twenty minutes   two hours   three days

Think About It — Fact or Opinion

A **fact** is a true statement. An **opinion** is a statement that tells what a person thinks. Write **F** beside each statement that is a fact. Write **O** beside each statement that is an opinion.

_____ 1. Sandstorms are worse than snowstorms.

_____ 2. There is a lot of loose sand on the desert floor.

_____ 3. Mohammed Selim's parents should not have let him go outside that day.

_____ 4. It is easier to ride a bicycle than a donkey.

_____ 5. Some people were hurt when large signs blew over.

_____ 6. People found it hard to breathe during the storm.

Focus on Vocabulary — Find the Meaning

Read each sentence. Circle the best meaning for the word in dark print.

1. Wind carried sand from nearby **deserts**.
   beaches   dry land that gets little rain   holes

2. Selim had lived through several small **sandstorms**.
   storms of blowing sand   hot, dry weather   floods

3. The wind picked up more than a **ton** of sand.
   2,000 pounds   barrel   mile

4. The **visibility** was zero in the blowing sand.
   size   warning   distance something can be seen

5. Most sandstorms were a **nuisance**.
   danger   something that bothers people   target

6. The wind **threatened** to pick people up.
   howled   moved   gave signs of doing harm

7. Many Egyptians held onto things that were **anchored**.
   tied down   loosened   buried

8. Sand and **debris** flew through the air.
   birds   bits of broken things   clothing

9. Some people ran under a **balcony**.
   low bridge   ladder   raised porch

10. The wind **uprooted** trees.
    tore   shook   pulled up

Sand Dunes

Sand **dunes** form as wind moves sand. The wind picks up some sand and carries it a few feet away. Then it drops the sand. Over time, the sand begins to build up. Then it creates a dune. Study the diagram below. Circle the answer to each question.

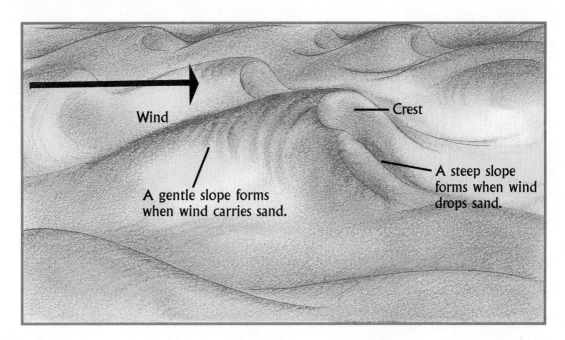

Wind

Crest

A gentle slope forms when wind carries sand.

A steep slope forms when wind drops sand.

1. What is a sand dune?

a desert storm   a hill of sand   a desert pond

2. Where is the crest of a sand dune?

the bottom   the side   the top

3. What is a slope?

a slant   a sandstorm   a gentle breeze

4. What causes a dune to have a gentle slope?

the wind   the sun   new sand

5. What forms when wind drops sand?

a steep slope   a stronger breeze   a gentle slope

Tornado Rips Through Texas Town

Maria Ruiz knew that a tornado was coming. So did most other people in Jarrell, Texas. They heard about it on the radio on May 27, 1997. The town **siren** also blasted a warning.

Ruiz lived in a **mobile** home. She knew her lightweight home could easily be picked up and smashed by the fierce wind. So she and her two teenage sons headed for the Moehrings' house. The Moehrings lived in a large, two-story home. Ruiz thought she and her boys would be safer there.

Trouble on the Way

The people of Jarrell had seen tornadoes before. In fact, one had hit the town in 1989. That twister left one person dead and damaged many homes. But this one was much worse. It was rated an F-5. That rating meant that the storm was very powerful. In fact, it was one of the strongest tornadoes ever. Its winds were **rotating** at more than 260 miles per hour. Winds this strong could pull the tar off a road. They could lift a house into the air. They could even rip the hair off a cow's back.

With the threatening tornado on the way, everyone in Jarrell looked for a safe place to hide. But there weren't many good spots. Most of the homes did not have basements or other underground hiding places. Some people ran to the middle of their houses. That at least got them away from the windows. Other people huddled in their bathrooms. There, they hid in bathtubs. Bathtubs have pipes that run into the ground. During a tornado, these pipes help keep bathtubs anchored in place. A bathtub is usually the last thing in a house to get blown away.

By early afternoon, the tornado could be seen on the **horizon**. It was huge. Most tornadoes are only a few hundred feet wide. This one was three thousand feet wide! The sky above it was a **mass** of black clouds. "That sky was as black as night," said Bud Taylor, a person from Jarrell.

The tornado was spinning wildly. But it wasn't moving toward the town very fast. Its forward speed was only about 20 miles per hour. Bud Taylor said, "It seemed like it sat there for 10 minutes making up its mind which way to go." Finally, around 3:45 P.M., the tornado moved into Jarrell. It struck a part of town called Double Creek Estates.

Lucky and Unlucky

For Bud Taylor, the tornado's path meant good news. His home was not hit. But other people in town were not so lucky. The twister blasted through Ronnie Tonn's farm. Its strong, swirling winds ripped the

This house was caught in the path of the Jarrell twister.

The F-5 tornado destroyed many homes in the town of Jarrell, Texas.

wheat out of his fields. The tornado blew the roof off his buildings. It carried away all 230 of his cows.

From the Tonn farm, the tornado moved along the edge of County Road 305. It barely touched one side of the road. But it blasted everything on the other side. There, 50 homes were destroyed completely.

Virginia Davidson was in one of these homes. When she saw the tornado coming, she thought for sure she was going to die. Davidson jumped into her bathtub. She threw a blanket over her head. She lay there as the strong wind blew her house to bits. The tornado ripped apart the roof and walls. It swept up everything inside the house. Davidson felt the bathtub being lifted into the air. The wind carried her 100 feet. Then it threw her back to the ground. **Amazingly**, Davidson walked away with just a few cuts. She was lucky to have her life. Everything else Virginia Davidson had was gone.

Mobile homes

The Wrong Place to Hide

For Maria Ruiz and her sons, the tornado's path meant **disaster**. The tornado **veered** away from the mobile home they had left. The Ruiz home was left standing. Instead, the tornado struck the Moehring house with its full force. Everyone inside died. That included four members of the Moehring family. That also included Maria, John, and Michael Ruiz.

After the tornado passed, friends and neighbors hurried to the places that had been hit. They wanted to see if **survivors** could be found. Tracy Burke went to the Moehrings. "We wanted to see if there was any way they could have made it," he said. "When we got there, the **foundation** was the only thing left."

Foundations were the only signs that some houses had ever been there. Everything else was gone. The same was true of other homes, as well. Double Creek Estates was "pretty well flattened," said one police officer. "It looked like a bomb had exploded," added high school principal John Johnson.

The tornado was one of the worst ever in Texas. In all, it killed 27 people. It caused 20 million dollars in damage. Still, the people of Jarrell did not give up on their town. They went to work rebuilding it. "It was so pretty before," said Charlene Adams. "But it will be pretty again."

The people of Jarrell work to rebuild their town.

Read and Remember — Choose the Answer

Draw a circle around the correct answer.

1. Where did Maria Ruiz and her sons go?

   the Moehrings' house   the school   Bud Taylor's store

2. What was this tornado rated?

   F-5   category 1   T-10

3. Where did Virginia Davidson hide?

   in her basement   in a closet   in the bathtub

4. What did Ronnie Tonn lose in the tornado?

   his car   all his cows   his hat

5. What happened to the Moehrings' house?

   It was destroyed.   It was not harmed.   It tipped over.

Write About It

Imagine you have just lived through the Jarrell tornado.
Write a short journal entry describing the day.

Focus on Vocabulary — Make a Word

Choose a word in dark print to complete each sentence. Write the letters of the word on the blanks. When you are finished, the letters in the circles will tell what kind of home the Moehrings had.

siren	**veered**	**mass**	**rotating**
horizon	**survivors**	**mobile**	**amazingly**
disaster	**foundation**		

1. Maria Ruiz lived in a _____ home.

◯ _ _ _ _ _ _

2. The tornado's winds were _____ around and around.

_ _ _ ◯ _ _ _ _

3. The town _____ blew a warning.

_ ◯ _ _ _

4. Virginia Davidson _____ lived through the tornado.

_ _ ◯ _ _ _ _ _ _

5. The tornado _____ away from the Ruiz's mobile home.

_ _ ◯ _ _ _

6. The tornado could be seen on the _____.

_ ◯ _ _ _ _ _

7. After the tornado, people looked for _____.

_ _ ◯ _ _ _ _ _ _

8. Only the _____ remained of the Moehrings' house.

_ _ ◯ _ _ _ _ _ _ _

9. The sky was a _____ of black clouds.

_ ◯ _ _

10. For Maria Ruiz, the tornado's path meant _____.

_ _ _ ◯ _ _ _ _

SCIENCE CONNECTION

Comparing Tornadoes

🌀 The **Fujita scale** is a chart that compares the strengths of **tornadoes**. A tornado is **rated** by its wind speed and its effects. Study the chart below. Write the answer to each question.

Fujita Scale		
Tornado	Wind Speeds (in miles per hour)	Effects
F-0	40–72	Damages chimneys, trees, and signs.
F-1	73–112	Pushes cars off the road. Turns over light homes.
F-2	113–157	Tears off roofs. Tears apart light homes. Breaks large trees.
F-3	158–206	Turns over trains. Breaks most trees. Tears off roofs and walls from most houses.
F-4	207–260	Tears apart strong houses. Throws cars. Carries light buildings.
F-5	More than 261	Lifts and tears apart strong houses. Cars fly through the air.

1. What is the Fujita scale? _____

_____

2. What wind speeds can an F-2 tornado have? _____

3. Which kind of tornado can have a wind speed of 200 miles per hour? _____

4. Which is stronger—an F-3 or an F-4 tornado? _____

5. What are the effects of an F-1 tornado? _____

6. Which tornado can lift strong houses? _____

Trouble in the Sky

Hiroaki Hanai was on his way to Hawaii. His elderly parents, Yoko and Shigeru Hanai, were with him. The Hanais left Tokyo, Japan, on December 28, 1997. About nine that night, they boarded Flight 826. As the plane headed out across the Pacific Ocean, Hiroaki settled back in his seat. He knew it would be a long flight. So he wanted to try to get some sleep. He expected to be in Hawaii in about six hours. But on this night, things did not go according to plan.

A Quiet Start

Shortly after the plane took off, flight attendants served dinner. They handed out trays of food. They also poured drinks for people. There were 374 passengers on board that night. So the 19 crew members were kept very busy. Two hours into the flight, they were still working to clear away all the dinner trays.

By then, many passengers had taken off their seat belts. Several people had gotten up to stretch their legs or use the restroom. Others just felt better with their seat belts off. There seemed to be no reason to stay belted. The flight was not at all bumpy. In fact, it was very smooth.

Up in the front of the plane, the pilot thought everything looked good. The plane's **instruments** showed no bad weather ahead. The night sky looked very calm.

But suddenly, something went wrong. The plane hit a tremendous wave of air. This wind pushed the jet up higher into the sky. A few seconds later, another blast of wind slammed the jet back down. Winds like these might have been expected during a storm, but the sky was clear.

The plane had hit **clear air turbulence**. That is a strange kind of air movement. It comes from two strong gusts of wind bumping into each other. Usually, this only happens during storms. But as the passengers of Flight 826 learned, it can happen when the sky is perfectly clear, too.

Strong Winds

When the trouble struck, the plane was traveling at an **altitude** of 31,000 feet. It was up in the **jet stream**. That is a stream of air that circles the earth. The jet stream blows from west to east. Planes traveling east often fly in this jet stream. If planes enter this stream of air, the wind there can help push them along, making them go faster.

Flight 826 was in the jet stream. But all at once, the plane hit strong waves of air going in different directions. Those waves of air caused the clear air

The bouncing plane threw many objects and people into the air.

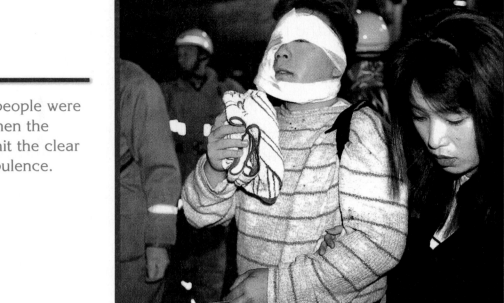

Many people were hurt when the plane hit the clear air turbulence.

turbulence. This made it hard for the pilot to keep the plane steady. The plane was being bounced between the waves of air.

For people in the plane, the sudden **updraft** was a shock. Passengers felt they were being pushed hard into their seats. The **downdraft** that followed was even worse. The plane fell about 1,000 feet in the blink of an eye. People felt as if their seats had dropped out from under them. "It was as though the plane dipped in a **free fall** beneath us, leaving our bodies behind," said Hiroaki Hanai.

Anyone not wearing a seat belt was thrown into the air. Dozens of people hit the ceiling. Many banged their heads on the overhead bins. Food and drinks went flying. Glasses smashed against the ceiling. Forks, knives, bags, and books flew everywhere. People's suitcases, shoes, and purses went flying, too.

"I thought I was dying," said Kiyotaka Eto. Hiroaki Hanai's 70-year-old mother, Yoko, had the same thought. She was one of the ones thrown from her seat. Her head hit the ceiling hard. "So this is what a plane crash feels like," she thought to herself.

Back to Japan

As the plane **leveled** off, some people fell to the floor. Some were hurt when they fell. Others were cut by pieces of flying glass. One woman, Konomi Kataura, was knocked **unconscious**. A doctor on the plane crawled forward to help her. But there was nothing he could do. Kataura soon died from her **injuries**.

Ten seconds after hitting the clear air turbulence, the pilot was able to straighten out the plane. The plane left the wild waves of air behind. But by then, the inside of the plane was a mess. People were lying on the floor. Many people were bleeding. Glass, food, and other debris lay everywhere. Part of the plane's ceiling had fallen in.

The pilot quickly turned the plane around. Instead of flying on to Hawaii, Flight 826 returned to Japan. There, 83 people were taken to the hospital. Nine of them were flight attendants. Hiroaki Hanai and his parents walked away with no serious injuries. Yoko Hanai's head hurt for several days afterward. But as her husband said, "At least we are safe."

Many passengers were taken to the hospital after Flight 826 returned to Japan.

USE WHAT YOU KNOW

Read and Remember — Check the Events

Place a check in front of the three sentences that tell what happened in the story.

_____ **1.** Flight 826 flew through a bad storm.

_____ **2.** Hiroaki Hanai took his parents to China.

_____ **3.** Some people on the plane took off their seat belts.

_____ **4.** The plane hit a strong blast of wind.

_____ **5.** The pilot died trying to help Hiroaki Hanai.

_____ **6.** Instead of flying to Hawaii, Flight 826 returned to Japan.

Think About It — Drawing Conclusions

Write one or more sentences to answer each question.

1. Why do you think some people on the plane got up to stretch their legs?_____

_____

2. Why were people surprised when the plane was pushed higher up into the sky?_____

_____

3. Why were 83 people taken to the hospital?_____

_____

4. Why do you think Yoko Hanai's head hurt for several days afterward?_____

_____

Focus on Vocabulary — Match Up

Match each word with its meaning. Darken the circle beside the correct answer.

1. instruments
  ○ televisions   ○ windows   ○ tools used to fly a plane

2. clear air turbulence
  ○ sudden bursts of wind   ○ clouds   ○ runways

3. altitude
  ○ level of heat   ○ height above sea level   ○ sound

4. jet stream
  ○ landing   ○ air that circles the earth   ○ airport

5. updraft
  ○ air moving upward   ○ explosion   ○ warning

6. downdraft
  ○ landing   ○ air moving downward   ○ power

7. free fall
  ○ open lane   ○ a fall through space   ○ trip

8. leveled
  ○ stopped going up and down   ○ burned   ○ turned

9. unconscious
  ○ not helpful   ○ not happy   ○ not awake

10. injuries
  ○ fights   ○ harm to the body   ○ decisions

How an Airplane Flies

Each part of an airplane is important for it to fly, turn, or land. One part is the **rudder**, which helps control the airplane as it turns. Other important parts are the **elevators**. They help the airplane go up or down. Study the airplane diagram below. Circle the answer that best completes each sentence.

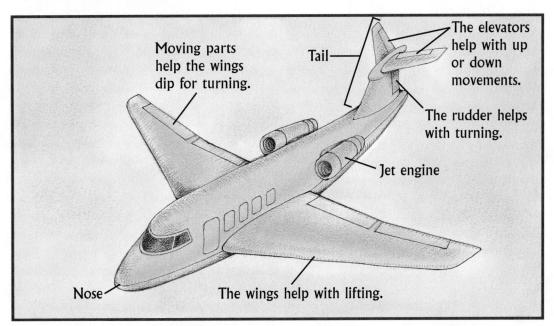

Moving parts help the wings dip for turning.

Tail

The elevators help with up or down movements.

The rudder helps with turning.

Jet engine

The wings help with lifting.

Nose

1. The front of an airplane is the _____.
   rudder   tail   nose

2. The _____ helps an airplane turn.
   jet engine   nose   rudder

3. Elevators help an airplane _____.
   go up or down   go fast   turn

4. An airplane's _____ help it lift into the air.
   noses   wings   rudders

5. The back of an airplane is called the _____.
   tail   jet engine   wing

Killer Wind from the Sea

Trouble was coming, but Saira Ahemad didn't know it. Neither did anyone else at the Kandla **salt mines**. Ahemad was one of 20,000 workers at the salt mines in Kandla, India. Hour after hour, the workers used their bare hands to scrape salt off the ground. They put it into piles so it could be packed and shipped. They did this every day. So for them, there was nothing special about June 8, 1998. They didn't know a terrible storm was about to wipe out everything around them.

A Storm on the Way

The storm began in the Arabian Sea. Cold dry air from the north met warm, wet air from the south. A **front** formed between the cold air and the warm air. Along the front, rain and wind **developed**. The wind swirled faster and faster. Soon it became a hurricane. In this part of the world, however, it was not called a hurricane. It was called a **cyclone**.

The cyclone headed toward the western coast of India. It carried winds of 75 miles per hour. The winds whipped along the top of the water, making huge waves. The waves headed for the coast, too.

By 5 P.M. on June 8, some people in Kandla had heard that a bad storm was coming. Ship owners hurried to **protect** their ships. Business owners rushed to close down their buildings. But no one thought to warn the workers in the salt mines.

The salt mines had always been huge flat fields of mud at the very edge of the Arabian Sea. Every few hours, waves of salty seawater would wash over

Workers in the salt mines would gather salt left in the mud.

these fields. The hot sun would **evaporate** the water quickly. Then **pure** salt would be left in the mud. Workers would then gather up the salt before the next waves of salty seawater would come.

Working in the salt mines was tiring and hard, and it did not pay well. So whole families often worked together to make their living. Saira Ahemad worked with her sister and four other family members at the salt mines. Together they barely made enough money to survive.

Rising Wind

On June 8, Ahemad and her family put in a long day of work. By that evening, the wind was rising. Ahemad didn't think much about it, though. She was too tired. She went to bed in a little wooden hut next to the salt mines. Thousands of other workers did the same.

All night, the wind blew through Ahemad's hut. By morning on June 9, it was growing stronger. Still,

Ahemad and the other workers went out to gather salt. The more salt they gathered, the more money they made. They couldn't afford to worry about the weather. Besides, these workers were not aware that a huge storm was coming.

By noon, the cyclone was near the coast. Its winds were up to 100 miles per hour. The blowing wind formed giant waves in the sea. Some of the waves were over 30 feet high. In the early afternoon, the wind pushed these waves **directly** at the Kandla salt mines.

Driven by the high wind, the waves crashed down on the salt mines. They smashed hundreds of wooden huts to pieces. They washed away one and a half million tons of salt. The waves also swept thousands of people out into the Arabian Sea.

Sad Times

Saira Ahemad was lucky. When the waves hit, she and many others **scrambled** toward a tall building. She pushed and fought against the wind and water. At last, she and some of the others made it safely to

The salt mines were flat fields of mud at the edge of the Arabian Sea.

the building. Saira Ahemad survived. But her family members were washed out to sea, never to be seen again.

Yogesh Patel was another survivor. He grabbed a pole that was sticking out of the ground. For eight long hours he held on to that pole. The wind and water swirled around him. Yet he managed to hang on. Said Patel, "I saw people being washed into the sea, small children who could not save themselves."

By 4:30 that afternoon, the wind was slowing down. The waves and the rain were also dying down. But by then, the damage was done. More than 10,000 people were missing. Many would never be found. Their bodies had **disappeared** into the Arabian Sea.

Survivors were filled with sadness. "My heart is broken," sobbed Saira Ahemad. Others felt the same way. Nan Bai lost her four sons and a daughter in the cyclone. She stood with tears streaming down her face. "It took my everything," she said.

Yet even as they cried, many survivors got ready to go back to work. One such person was Nanbai Gopal. She lost five family members in the cyclone. But when asked what she planned to do next, she held up her hands. "I will work," she said. "I am strong."

A survivor waits to leave the area the cyclone hit.

Read and Remember — Finish the Sentence

Circle the best ending for each sentence.

1. Working in the salt mines was _____.
   exciting   noisy   tiring

2. The workers were not told about the _____.
   ship   storm   mud

3. The storm brought _____.
   cold temperatures   strong wind   blowing sand

4. When the storm came, the workers were _____.
   in bed   in the dining hall   in the salt mines

5. Many people were _____.
   crushed   washed away   safe in huts

Write About It

Imagine you are a newspaper reporter. Write a short news article about the Kandla salt mines. In your article, tell who, what, when, where, and why.

75

Focus on Vocabulary — Finish the Paragraphs

Use the words in dark print to complete the paragraphs. Reread the paragraphs to be sure they make sense.

directly	**evaporate**	**scrambled**	**disappeared**
protect	**cyclone**	**front**	**pure**
developed	**salt mines**		

On June 8, 1998, a weather **(1)**_____ formed when cold air and warm air met over the Arabian Sea. Rain and wind **(2)**_____. As the winds grew stronger, the storm became a **(3)**_____. It headed for the Kandla **(4)**_____. The workers there had no way to **(5)**_____ themselves. They didn't even know the storm was coming. So they kept working in the fields. On most days, the hot sun would **(6)**_____ the salty seawater. Then the workers would quickly gather up the **(7)**_____ salt left behind.

On June 9, the strong storm hit. Its winds blew **(8)**_____ at the workers. Some of the workers **(9)**_____ to safety. But thousands of others **(10)**_____ in the sea. They were never seen again.

Storm Names

Sometimes a dangerous storm with strong winds begins over warm ocean waters. It is called a **hurricane**, **cyclone**, **typhoon**, or **willy-willy**, depending on where it occurs. Study the map of storms below. The **map key** tells which color is used for a storm name. Write the answer to each question.

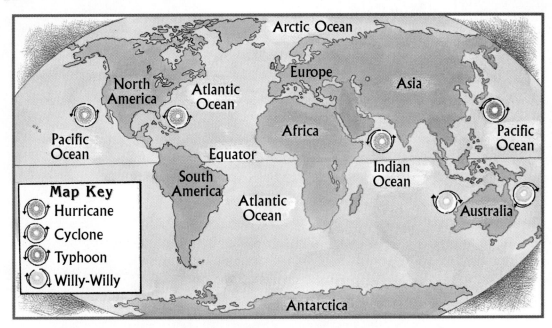

1. How many different names are used for the storms?

   2   4   8

2. What color is used to show a hurricane?

   green   yellow   red

3. What is the name of a storm near Australia?

   willy-willy   hurricane   typhoon

4. Over which ocean does a cyclone occur?

   Indian Ocean   Atlantic Ocean   Pacific Ocean

5. What storm can form over the Pacific Ocean near Asia?

   typhoon   hurricane   cyclone

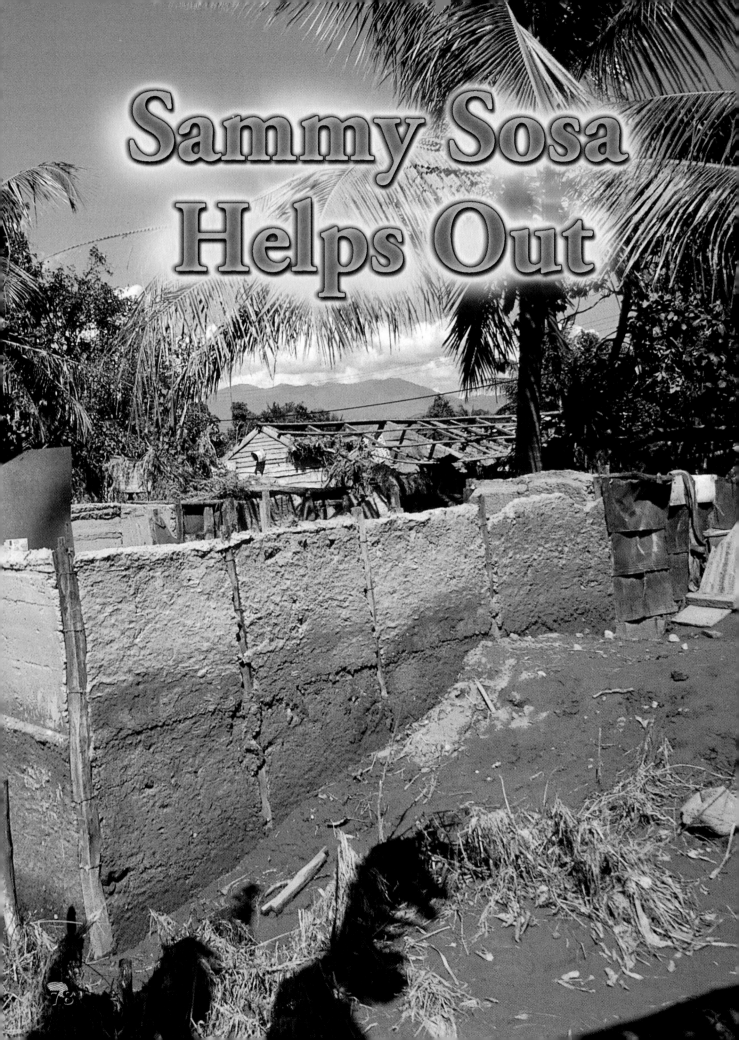

Sammy Sosa Helps Out

Sammy Sosa was in a **slump**. He hadn't hit a home run in five games. For most baseball players, that wouldn't be a slump. But Sammy Sosa of the Chicago Cubs wasn't just any player. In 1998 he and Mark McGwire of the St. Louis Cardinals were having the greatest home run battle of all time. But on September 22, Sosa was stuck at 63 home runs.

Baseball was not the only thing on Sosa's mind. He was worried about a storm near the Dominican Republic in the Caribbean Sea. The storm was called Hurricane Georges.

Bad News

Sosa had grown up in the Dominican Republic. He had friends and family members still living on the island. So he was very worried when he heard that Hurricane Georges was headed that way.

Meteorologists, scientists who study weather, did not think Hurricane Georges would do much damage to the Dominican Republic. They thought the storm would just brush the north coast. But at the last moment, the hurricane changed **course**. Georges ripped across the island with a wind of 110 miles per hour.

Like other large hurricanes, this one caused great damage. Some of the trouble came from flooding. Most of the damage came from the wind. Its **velocity** was very strong. It blew the roof off the baseball park in Sosa's **hometown**. It bent the light poles. It even blew over the outfield wall.

Hurricane Georges left nearly 100,000 people of the Dominican Republic without homes. It killed more than

200 people. It ruined most of the island's crops. That left many farmers without a way to make a living.

A Hometown Hero

When Sammy Sosa heard that Hurricane Georges had hit the Dominican Republic, he knew that he wanted to help. He raised money for the survivors. They needed food, clothing, and places to live. Sosa also tried to bring a bit of happiness to these people during a time of much sadness. He knew that most Dominicans loved baseball. They cheered him as their hometown hero. So Sosa thought that if he could hit more home runs, that would give them something to smile about.

The next day, September 23, Sosa broke out of his slump. He hit his 64th and 65th home runs. He **dedicated** these home runs to the Dominican people. "I am at the side of all Dominicans, of my people, of my **nation**," he said. "Hopefully, these home runs will bring a little happiness."

Indeed, news of Sosa's home runs thrilled Dominicans. When they heard the news, they

Hurricane Georges caused great damage when it hit the Dominican Republic.

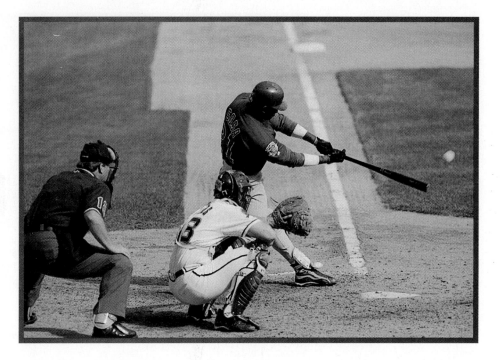

Sammy Sosa dedicated two home runs to the Dominican Republic.

cheered, clapped, and honked their horns. One local newspaper headline read, "65!" Even with their island in shambles, these people were keeping track of Sosa's home-run battle.

Doing His Best

Sammy Sosa finished the baseball season with 66 home runs. That left him four behind Mark McGwire. Sosa didn't mind that he didn't win the home-run battle. Instead, he was named Most Valuable Player for the National League. This made Sosa very happy. But he still had a lot on his mind. He couldn't help thinking about the people of the Dominican Republic.

Even before Hurricane Georges hit, Sosa had done a lot for the Dominican Republic. He had built a baseball field and a shopping center. He had given computers to schools. He had brought in machines to **purify** water. So after Hurricane Georges struck, the survivors again looked to Sosa for help.

"We are his people," said Eduardo Torreano, who grew up with Sosa. "He hasn't forgotten us. Sammy will come back soon, and he will help."

After the hurricane, Sosa returned to the Dominican Republic.

Torreano was right. Sosa did everything he could to help the people of the Dominican Republic. He arranged to send 60,000 pounds of food to the island. He sent safe drinking water in bottles. Sosa also helped raise nearly half a million dollars. The money would be used to help people rebuild their homes.

On October 20, Sammy Sosa returned to the Dominican Republic. Even in the rain, people came out to greet him. They lined the road leading to his hometown. Some had the number "66" painted on their car windows. Others held signs that read, "Welcome to your country, Sammy!"

Sosa told the people that he would continue to help them. He told them that many **supplies** were already on the way. He told them that three planes and six boats filled with food and medicine would be coming soon.

These supplies were important. They would help the people of the Dominican Republic rebuild their lives. This brought much gladness and **relief**. But for many people, just having Sosa there made them feel good. As Alfredo Griffin put it, "He brings happiness to the country."

Read and Remember — Choose the Answer

Draw a circle around the correct answer.

1. Where did Sammy Sosa grow up?

Chicago   St. Louis   Dominican Republic

2. What caused most of the damage during Hurricane Georges?

forest fires   strong winds   high waves

3. What kind of battle were Sammy Sosa and Mark McGwire in?

a pitching battle   a home-run battle   a catching battle

4. What did Sosa send to the Dominican Republic?

new cars   baseball equipment   food and medicine

5. Why did Hurricane Georges surprise meteorologists?

It changed course.   It was small.   It caused floods.

Think About It — Find the Sequence

Number the sentences to show the correct order from the story. The first one is done for you.

_____ **1.** Sammy Sosa was named Most Valuable Player.

_____ **2.** Hurricane Georges blew through the Caribbean Sea.

__1__ **3.** Sammy Sosa built a baseball field in the Dominican Republic.

_____ **4.** People painted the number "66" on their car windows.

_____ **5.** Sammy Sosa hit his 64th and 65th home runs.

Focus on Vocabulary — Crossword Puzzle

Use the clues to complete the puzzle. Choose from the words in dark print.

meteorologists   velocity   purify   supplies   course
dedicated   slump   nation   relief   hometown

Across

4. speed
5. freedom from sadness
7. scientists who study weather
9. did in honor of something
10. make clean or pure

Down

1. where someone grew up
2. group of people with their own government
3. a period of not doing something well
6. a path
8. needed things

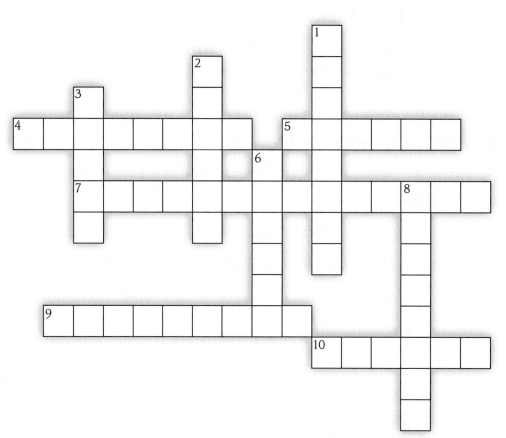

Weather Map

A **weather map** shows what kind of weather to expect in an area. The map below shows one day's weather in the United States, Canada, and Mexico. The **map key** explains what the symbols or colors on the map mean. Study the map. Circle the answer to each question.

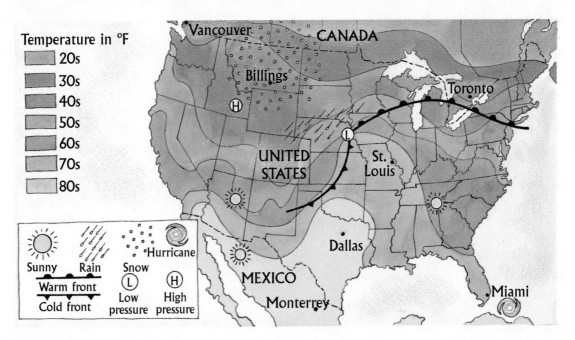

1. Which is the symbol for a hurricane?

    ⒣   ☔   🌀

2. What color is used to show a temperature of 65°F?
   dark green   dark blue   orange

3. What is the weather like in Billings?
   sunny   rainy   snowy

4. Which city has about the same temperature as Monterrey?
   Dallas   Vancouver   St. Louis

5. Which city is in danger from a hurricane?
   Toronto   Miami   Dallas

A Deadly Day in South Africa

elson Mandela was on vacation. Mandela was the president of South Africa. He spent much of the year in the city. But in December 1998, he returned to his home village of Qunu. He planned to rest for a while before going back to work.

On December 15, Mandela decided to do some shopping. He went to Umtata. This was a small farming town twelve miles from his home. The town was quiet when Mandela got there. But that would soon change.

No Warning

In Umtata, the 80-year-old Mandela went into a **pharmacy**. As he walked through the store, a few reporters were with him. So were his **bodyguards**. The bodyguards had the job of protecting Mandela from harm. At any moment, someone might try to hurt the president. So these bodyguards were always watching out for trouble.

On this day, no person threatened Mandela. But a different kind of danger was building. It began as a bad thunderstorm far to the west. There, thunder and **lightning** filled the sky. Suddenly, a tube of swirling wind came down from the clouds. It was a tornado.

Within minutes, the tornado moved in on Umtata. It traveled with frightening speed. Most tornadoes travel across the sky at about 30 to 40 miles per hour. This one was moving much faster. When it reached the town at 3 P.M., it was moving at 75 miles per hour. That meant it was moving about as fast as cars speeding down a highway. There was no way people

Nelson Mandela was the president of South Africa.

could get out of its way. The tornado surprised the people in Umtata.

Mandela had no idea the tornado was coming. Neither did anyone else. But suddenly, the storm hit. "We just heard a rattle, and the ceiling started **vibrating**," said one reporter. A few seconds later, the building seemed to explode. The wind blew the glass out of the windows. It tore apart the roof. It caused part of the store to **collapse**.

Mandela didn't know what was happening. Neither did his bodyguards. They thought a bomb was going off. So these brave men threw themselves on top of the president. They pushed him to the floor. They used their own bodies to protect him, hoping that would keep him safe.

Clouds, Ice, and Wind

Elsewhere in Umtata, other people were also caught in the terrible twister. Some saw a sudden darkness fall over the town. The black clouds at the top of the tornado blocked out the sun. "I was in a car when a cloud covered the town," said Lawrence Nkosi. "I couldn't see anything."

Next, Nkosi heard **hail** falling all around him. This hail was made up of hard pieces of ice and snow. It fell from the clouds surrounding the tornado. The hail was formed when drops of water in the clouds above got caught in moving air. The drops of water were carried up into very cold air. There, they froze into ice, making hail. The heavy hail fell to the earth during the storm.

The tornado moved so quickly that few people had time to take cover. Some were waiting at a bus stop. There was a wall behind them. The tornado smashed into the wall and pushed it over, killing eleven people. Others were killed when the tornado blew apart a store.

The swirling wind destroyed everything in its path. Stores and houses were left without roofs. Traffic lights and telephone poles were twisted and broken. Hundreds of trees were uprooted and blown across the town.

Stan Mzimba was a reporter in Umtata. "I've never seen anything like it," he said. "I've never seen such a

The black clouds at the top of the tornado blocked out the sun.

disaster before." Mzimba said that the whole town looked like a battle **zone**.

A Killer Storm

When Mandela's bodyguards realized what was happening, they continued to **shield** him. They waited until the tornado was gone. Then they helped him to his feet. Mandela was not hurt. But two of his bodyguards were. They had been cut by pieces of flying glass. They needed stitches to close the cuts.

Luckily, the bodyguards were not badly hurt. But many others were. They were taken to Umtata General Hospital for **treatment**. Everything there was in **turmoil**. The hospital itself had been damaged by the tornado. Half of its roof had been blown off.

In all, 18 people lost their lives in the tornado. About 163 people were seriously hurt. In just a few minutes, the wind had caused 200 million dollars in damages. It would be a long time before the people of Umtata would forget this killer tornado. It would also be a long time before Nelson Mandela and his bodyguards would forget this surprise storm.

One reporter said that Umtata looked like a battle zone after the tornado.

Read and Remember — Check the Events

Place a check in front of the three sentences that tell what happened in the story.

_____ **1.** Nelson Mandela went swimming in Umtata.

_____ **2.** A tornado struck the building where Mandela was shopping.

_____ **3.** A man tried to attack Mandela.

_____ **4.** Mandela's guards pushed him to the floor to protect him.

_____ **5.** The tornado killed 18 people.

_____ **6.** Only the hospital made it through the tornado without damage.

Write About It

Imagine you are one of Nelson Mandela's bodyguards. Write a letter to a friend, describing how you felt when the tornado struck.

Dear _____,

_____

_____

_____

_____

_____

_____

_____

_____

_____

Focus on Vocabulary — Make a Word

Choose a word in dark print to complete each sentence. Write the letters of the word on the blanks. When you are finished, the letters in the circles will tell the name of a reporter who was in Umtata with Nelson Mandela.

pharmacy	bodyguards	lightning	vibrating
collapse	hail	zone	shield
treatment	turmoil		

1. Mandela's guards tried to _____ him.
   ○ _ _ _ _ _ _

2. Thunder and _____ filled the sky.
   _ _ _ _ ○ _ _ _ _

3. Mandela's _____ had gone in with him.
   _ _ _ _ _ _ ○ _ _ _

4. Many people went to the hospital for _____.
   _ _ _ _ ○ ○ _ _ _ _

5. Everything was in a messy _____.
   _ _ _ ○ _ _ _

6. One reporter said Umtata looked like a disaster _____.
   _ ○ _ _

7. Nkosi heard _____ falling all around him.
   _ ○ _ _

8. Mandela had gone into the _____.
   _ _ _ ○ _ _ _ _

9. The ceiling creaked when it started _____.
   _ _ _ ○ _ _ _ _ _

10. Part of the store began to _____ during the tornado.
    _ _ _ _ ○ _ _ _

How Wind Is Made

Air has weight, so it pushes down on Earth. Cold air weighs more than warm air, so it sinks. As cold air sinks, it pushes warm air up. The warm air cools as it rises. This movement of cold air and warm air creates wind. Study the wind diagram below. Write the answer to each question.

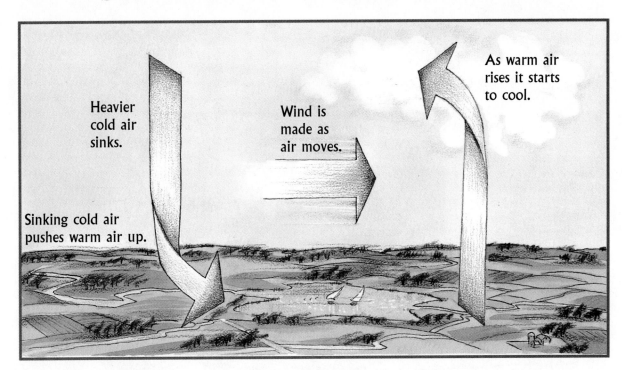

Heavier cold air sinks.

Wind is made as air moves.

As warm air rises it starts to cool.

Sinking cold air pushes warm air up.

1. Which is heavier—cold air or warm air? _____

2. What kind of air sinks? _____

3. What does cold air do to warm air? _____

_____

4. What is made by the movement of air? _____

5. What happens to warm air as it rises? _____

_____

Blown Away!

Amy Crago looked out the window. She saw a big black storm cloud moving toward the house. Crago knew what that meant. A tornado was on the way.

Crago lived in Grady County, Oklahoma. On May 3, 1999, several tornadoes swept through the area. They carried swirling winds of more than 260 miles per hour. People huddled together in their homes. Amy Crago hoped she would be safe at her parents' house. But when she saw the black cloud coming, she knew her family was in trouble.

No Time to Run

There was no time to get out of the house. Amy grabbed her 10-month-old daughter, Aleah. Then she and Aleah's father, Ben Crosby, hurried to the hall closet. They thought that would be the safest place to be. The closet had no windows so they would not get hit with pieces of broken glass. Amy's parents ran to the closet, too. The whole family sat close together. They hoped the walls wouldn't be blown down around them.

"As the storm got closer, it was very, very loud," said Amy. To her, it sounded like the roar of a jet engine. She also noticed a strong smell in the air. It came from trees and other wood houses being ripped apart. The smell was like freshly cut wood.

Minutes later, the tornado struck Amy's parents' house. It blew the roof right off. Amy, Ben, and Aleah were all pulled up into the air. Amy held on to Aleah as tightly as she could. But the force of the wind was simply too strong. The baby was ripped from her.

"I can't **pinpoint** when I let go of her," Amy said. "I just had her, and then I didn't."

The spinning tornado threw Amy against a tree. Again and again she was hit by flying pieces of debris. She put her head down and covered her face with her hands. "I'm going to die," she thought.

Hurt But Alive

At last, the wind died down. Amy slowly uncovered her face. The tornado was gone. Everything around her had been blown to bits. Amy herself had been thrown 100 feet. That is farther than the length of a basketball court.

She looked back toward her parents' house. It was no longer standing. The tornado had destroyed it. She didn't see Ben or her parents, either. Amy thought they had all been killed by the tornado. She thought her baby was dead, too.

In fact, Amy's mother had died in the fierce storm. But Amy's father survived. He pulled himself out of the **rubble**. He was in shock. His wife was dead, and everything was destroyed. He began calling for Amy. But she was too far away to hear him. Ben couldn't

On May 3, 1999, a tornado struck Grady County, Oklahoma.

The tornado made rubble of buildings in its path.

hear him, either. Ben had been blown farther than anyone. Although Ben would **recover**, he was very badly injured. Amy's father thought his whole family was dead.

Finally, there was little Aleah. The wind had thrown her down at the bottom of a tree. She was lying on a heap of chicken wire. She had a scratch on one leg and a slightly injured left **lung**. She was also covered with mud. But amazingly, she was alive. Somehow, she had survived the ride inside the killer tornado.

A Happy Ending

One of the first rescue workers on the scene was Robert Jolley. He was a **deputy sheriff** in Grady County. Jolley had seen the tornado swirling across the land. He had followed it in his car, looking for survivors.

Jolley saw Amy's father **staggering** down the road. He looked weak and **confused**. Jolley asked him if anyone else in the family had survived.

"No," Amy's father sadly said. "They're all dead."

As Jolley looked at the rubble, he thought Amy's father was probably right. Still, he decided to look among the trees at the edge of the field. That's where many pieces of the house had been blown. "I knew that if anybody was left alive, they'd be in that **tree line**," he said.

Jolley walked over to the trees. Suddenly, he noticed something. He saw a small movement nearby. Jolley said. "I didn't know what it was. It was so small, so **slight**."

He reached down and poked his hand around in a pile of debris. His fingers touched something warm. It was Aleah's leg. He quickly grabbed Aleah and picked her up. "When I rubbed the mud from her ears and eyes, only then did she start to cry," he said. "I never thought I'd be so happy to hear a baby screaming. I was just excited that she was alive."

Jolley was not the only one. Amy Crago was **overjoyed** to learn that her baby had survived. So was the rest of the family. In fact, all across the country, people cheered the news. The story of Amy and Aleah Crago reminded everyone that some disasters have happy endings.

Amy Crago was overjoyed that Robert Jolley had rescued Aleah.

Read and Remember — Finish the Sentence

Circle the best ending for each sentence.

1. When Amy saw the tornado coming, she grabbed her _____.

grandmother   daughter   father

2. The tornado killed Amy's _____.

father   husband   mother

3. Aleah Crago was thrown onto a heap of _____.

burning wood   chicken wire   broken glass

4. Robert Jolley followed the tornado _____.

on his computer   in his car   with an ambulance

5. Jolley saw Amy's father _____.

in a house   in a tree   walking down the road

Think About It — Find the Main Ideas

Underline the two most important ideas from the story.

1. A tornado ripped through Grady County, Oklahoma, on May 3, 1999.

2. Amy Crago smelled freshly cut wood as the tornado came near.

3. Ben Crosby was thrown even farther than Amy Crago.

4. Amy Crago was very lucky that her baby and most of her family lived through the tornado.

5. Aleah Crago was 10 months old at the time of the tornado.

Focus on Vocabulary — Finish Up

Choose the correct word or words in dark print to complete each sentence.

pinpoint	**confused**	**tree line**	**overjoyed**
slight	**staggering**	**rubble**	**deputy sheriff**
recover	**lung**		

1. To return to normal is to _____.

2. A _____ helps a sheriff enforce the laws.

3. To be unclear of what is going on is to be _____.

4. A _____ is where trees grow next to a field.

5. Rough broken pieces of things are called _____.

6. Something that is very small is _____.

7. A _____ is a part of the body used for breathing.

8. To be very happy is to be _____.

9. Moving slowly and unevenly is _____.

10. To find the exact time or place of something is to _____ it.

Tornado Numbers

Tornadoes occur in almost every state in the United States. The bar graph below compares the **average** number of tornadoes that Texas, Oklahoma, Kansas, and Nebraska get each year. Study the bar graph. Write the answer to each question.

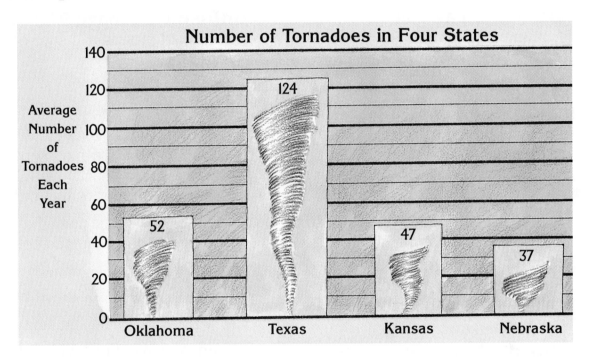

Number of Tornadoes in Four States

Average Number of Tornadoes Each Year

Oklahoma — 52
Texas — 124
Kansas — 47
Nebraska — 37

1. Which states are shown on the bar graph? _____

_____

2. What is Oklahoma's average number of tornadoes each year?

_____

3. Which state usually has the most tornadoes? _____

4. Which state usually gets more tornadoes—Kansas or Nebraska?

_____

5. Which state usually has the fewest tornadoes? _____

GLOSSARY

Words with this symbol can be found in the SCIENCE CONNECTION.

accident   page 34
An accident is a harmful event that is not expected.

accurate   page 31
Accurate means exactly right.

altitude   page 64
Altitude is height above sea level.

amazingly   page 57
Amazingly means surprisingly.

anchored   page 48
Anchored means tied down or held in place.

average   page 101
The average is the number or amount resulting from the division of the sum of quanities.

balcony   page 49
A balcony is like a porch with a railing built out from the side of a building.

blizzard   page 9
A blizzard is a heavy snowstorm with strong winds.

bodyguards   page 87
Bodyguards are people hired to protect a person from harm.

category   pages 23, 29
A category is one level or class.

chasers   page 31
Chasers are people who follow something, such as storms.

clear air turbulence   page 64
Clear air turbulence is strong bursts of wind bumping into each other.

coast   page 23
A coast is the seashore or the land close to a sea.

collapse   page 88
Collapse means to fall down.

confused   page 97
Confused means not sure of what is going on.

course   page 79
A course is a path.

cyclone   pages 71, 77
A cyclone is a strong storm that brings a great deal of rain. It is another name for a hurricane.

damage   page 24
Damage is harm caused by injury to one's body or property.

debris   page 49
Debris is broken pieces of material that are left after something has been destroyed or broken down.

dedicated   page 80
Dedicated means did in honor of something or someone.

degrees   page 7
Degrees are units of measure for temperature or distance.

dense   page 7
Dense means thick or very close together.

deputy sheriff   page 97
A deputy sheriff is a law officer that helps the sheriff.

deserts   page 47
Deserts are dry areas of land that get very little rain.

destroy   page 32
Destroy means ruin or tear apart.

developed   page 71
Developed means went through a process of forming.

directly   page 73
Directly means to move straight for something.

disappeared   page 74
Disappeared means moved out of sight.

disaster   page 57
A disaster is an event that happens suddenly and causes a lot of damage.

downdraft   page 65
A downdraft is a downward movement of air.

drought   page 8
A drought is a long time without any rain.

dunes   page 53
Dunes are rounded hills of windblown sand.

dust storm   page 8
A dust storm is a very strong wind that blows dust and dirt.

electricity   page 24
Electricity is a very strong form of power or energy. It is used to turn on lights in a building or house.

elements   page 41
Elements are different kinds of weather, such as rain, wind, and snow.

elevators   page 69
Elevators are part of an airplane. They help airplanes go up or down.

evaporate   page 72
Evaporate means to remove the wetness from something.

eye   page 42
The eye is the center of a hurricane. The air is calm in this part of the storm.

fiercely   page 9
Fiercely means strongly.

fleet   page 15
A fleet is group of ships.

force   page 41
Force is strength and power.

foundation   page 58
A foundation is the base on which a house is built.

free fall   page 65
A free fall is the fall of something through space.

front   page 71
A front is where two different types of weather or air masses come together.

Fujita scale   page 61
The Fujita scale is a chart that compares the strengths of tornadoes.

funnel   page 37
A funnel is a cone-shaped tube.

gushed   page 41
Gushed means flowed very quickly.

gusts   page 16

Gusts are sudden strong bursts of wind.

hail   page 89

Hail is small balls of ice that fall from clouds.

hillsides   page 26

Hillsides are the sides of hills.

hometown   page 79

A hometown is the place where a person was born or grew up.

horizon   page 56

The horizon is the line where it looks like the sky and the land meet.

huddled   page 40

Huddled means crowded together.

hurricane   pages 23, 29, 45, 77

A hurricane is a storm that has strong winds and usually occurs with rain, thunder, and lightning.

injuries   page 66

A person who has injuries is someone whose body has been hurt.

instruments   page 63

Instruments are tools used by a pilot to help fly an airplane.

jet stream   page 64

The jet stream is a stream of air that circles the earth.

leveled   page 66

Leveled means to have stopped going up and down.

life raft   page 18

A life raft is a small boat that people use in the water during an emergency.

lightning   page 87

Lightning is a flash of light made by a natural flow of electricity in the air.

lung   page 97

A lung is one of the two organs or parts of the body that breathe air.

map key   page 77, 85

A map key explains what the symbols or colors on a map mean.

mass   page 56

Mass means a large amount or number.

meteorologists   page 79

Meteorologists are scientists who study weather.

mobile   page 55

Mobile means able to be moved from place to place.

moist   page 8

Moist means a bit wet.

nation   page 80

A nation is a group of people who have their own government.

natural disaster   page 23

A natural disaster is a terrible event that is caused by nature, such as a flood or hurricane.

nervously   page 24

Nervously means in a way showing fear.

nuisance   page 48

A nuisance is something that bothers people.

officials   page 15

Officials are people who are in charge.

overjoyed   page 98
Overjoyed means very happy.

pharmacy   page 87
A pharmacy is a place where medicines are sold.

pinpoint   page 96
Pinpoint means to find the exact time or place of something.

pried   page 41
Pried means pulled apart with great strength.

protect   page 71
Protect means to guard or defend something from harm or damage.

pure   page 72
Pure means clean and not mixed with anything else.

purify   page 81
Purify means to make clean.

rated   pages 23, 61
Rated means placed into a class or level.

recover   page 97
Recover means to return to normal.

region   page 10
A region is an area of land.

relief   page 82
Relief means freedom from sadness or worry.

risk   page 15
Risk means possible danger.

rotating   page 55
Rotating means turning around a center or area.

rubble   page 96
Rubble is a large bunch of rough or broken stones or rocks.

rudder   page 69
A rudder is part of an airplane. It helps control the airplane as it turns.

salt mines   page 71
Salt mines are places where large amounts of salt are found.

sandstorms   page 47
Sandstorms are strong winds that blow sand.

scale   page 33
A scale is a standard of measurement.

scientists   page 31
Scientists are people who study one or more of the sciences.

scrambled   page 73
Scrambled means moved or climbed quickly.

shambles   page 42
A shambles is a big mess or ruins.

shattered   page 40
When something has shattered, it has broken into many pieces.

shield   page 90
Shield means to defend or keep from harm.

shift   page 17
A shift is a period of time when a person works.

shocked   page 42
Shocked means suddenly surprised and upset.

siren   page 55
A siren is a loud, shrill noise sounded to warn people of danger.

slight   page 98
Slight means very small, as in a movement or amount.

slump   page 79
A slump is a period of time of not doing something well.

spiral   page 31
A spiral is a curve that winds around and around.

squall   page 16
A squall is a small but strong storm.

staggering   page 97
Staggering means walking in a slow and shaky way.

struggled   page 18
Struggled means worked hard to do something or reach something.

supplies   page 82
Supplies are things needed for a certain use.

survived   page 42
Survived means stayed alive.

survivors   page 58
Survivors are people who lived through a disaster, such as a flood or an airplane crash.

swirling   page 9
Swirling means moving in circles.

temperature   page 7
Temperature is a measure of heat.

terrifying   page 25
Terrifying means very scary.

threatened   page 48
Threatened means to give signs of doing harm.

thundercloud   page 37
A thundercloud is a storm cloud that has thunder and lightning in it.

thunderstorm   pages 31, 45
A thunderstorm is a storm that occurs with thunder and lightning.

ton   page 47
A ton is a unit of weight. One ton is 2,000 pounds.

tornadoes   pages 31, 37, 61, 101
Tornadoes are storms with strong spinning and whirling winds.

treatment   page 90
Treatment is medical care.

tree line   page 98
A tree line is where trees are growing in a line along the edge of a field.

tremendous   page 17
Tremendous means very big or powerful.

turmoil   page 90
Turmoil means a mess or disorder.

twisters   page 31
Twisters are small powerful windstorms. A twister is another name for a tornado.

typhoon   page 77
A typhoon is a strong storm that brings much rain. It usually begins over the western part of the Pacific Ocean. It is another name for a cyclone or hurricane.

unconscious   page 66

An unconscious person is one who is not awake.

updraft   page 65

An updraft is an upward movement of air.

uprooted   page 49

Uprooted means pulled up by the roots.

veered   page 57

Veered means turned or changed direction.

velocity   page 79

Velocity means speed.

vibrating   page 88

When something is vibrating, it is moving quickly back and forth in a trembling motion.

visibility   page 47

Visibility is the distance that something can be seen. At zero visibility, nothing can be seen at any distance.

weather map   page 85

A weather map shows the kind of weather to expect in an area.

willy-willy   page 77

A willy-willy is a strong storm that brings much rain. It usually begins over the waters near Australia. It is another name for a cyclone or hurricane.

windstorms   page 17

Windstorms are storms with very strong winds and not much rain.

wind vane   page 21

A wind vane is a flat piece of metal attached to a pole that sits up high in the air. The metal swings when the wind blows. It shows which way the wind is blowing.

zone   page 90

A zone is an area of land.

Did You Know?

Saturn

Jupiter

◀ What are winds like on other planets? The planet Saturn spins very fast, so its winds blow at speeds of more than 1,000 miles per hour. Jupiter, the largest planet, also has fast winds. In fact, it has a large red spot that is probably a hurricane-like storm. This storm is three times the size of Earth!

Have you ever enjoyed flying kites ▶ in the wind? Kites were created by the Chinese about 3,000 years ago. They used them for fishing and to help them scare enemies during wars. Many, many years later, kites helped people create airplanes and study weather. Today kites are used mostly for fun.

◀ Did you know that a tornado can form over water? This kind of tornado is called a waterspout. Some waterspouts have been known to pick up and carry fish and frogs. When the waterspouts moved to land, the fish and frogs rained down!

How are hurricanes named? ▶
Each year a list of 21 male
and female names, such as
Andrew or Betsy, is created for
the Atlantic Ocean and other
areas. The list is in alphabetical
order. Each name begins with
a different letter of the alphabet.
The letters Q, U, X, Y, and Z
are always skipped.

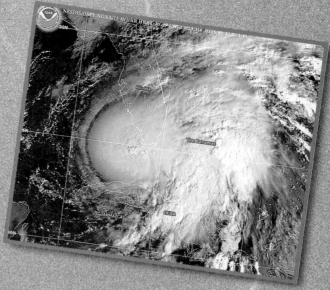

◀ What are some interesting
facts about tornadoes? The
heaviest item ever moved by
a tornado was a machine. It
weighed 30,000 pounds! One
tornado in England in 1950
even plucked the feathers
from chickens!

How have people used the ▶
power of wind? People first
used wind to sail boats. Later,
they created windmills in order
to pump water or to grind grain
for flour. In 1880 people first
used wind to create electricity.
Today huge windmills called
wind turbines create large
amounts of energy.

CHART YOUR SCORES

Score Your Work

1. Count the number of correct answers you have for each activity.
2. Write these numbers in the boxes in the chart.
3. Give yourself a score (maximum of 5 points) for **Write About It**.
4. Add up the numbers to get a final score for each tale.
5. Write your final score in the score box.
6. Compare your final score with the maximum score given for each story.

Tales	Read and Remember	Think About It	Write About It	Focus on Vocabulary	Science Connection	Score
Dust, Dust, and More Dust						/24
Tall Ship in Trouble						/23
High Winds Blast Jamaica						/25
Chasing the Wind						/23
September Surprise						/24
Sandstorm!						/26
Tornado Rips Through Texas Town						/26
Trouble in the Sky						/22
Killer Wind from the Sea						/25
Sammy Sosa Helps Out						/25
A Deadly Day in South Africa						/23
Blown Away!						/22

Dust, Dust, and More Dust

Pages 6–13

Read and Remember — Choose the Answer:
1. to clean them 2. chirp wildly 3. roller 4. by crawling 5. the Dust Bowl

Write About It: Answers will vary.

Focus on Vocabulary — Find the Meaning:
1. thick 2. measure of heat 3. units for measuring heat 4. wind that blows dust 5. lack of rain 6. a bit wet 7. heavy snowstorm 8. strongly 9. spinning 10. area of land

Science Connection — Causes of the Dust Bowl: 1. too little rain 2. ate plants 3. held soil in place 4. soil

Tall Ship in Trouble **Pages 14–21**

Read and Remember — Check the Events:
2, 3, 5

Think About It — Cause and Effect: 1. b 2. e 3. c 4. a 5. d

Focus on Vocabulary — Match Up: 1. people in charge 2. group of ships 3. danger 4. strong bursts of wind 5. small but strong storm 6. storms with strong winds 7. very big 8. work period 9. worked hard 10. small boat

Science Connection — Wind Direction:
1. A wind vane shows the direction from which wind blows. 2. south wind 3. from the north 4. east (E) 5. no

High Winds Blast Jamaica **Pages 22–29**

Read and Remember — Finish the Sentence:
1. hurricane warnings 2. Atlantic Ocean 3. five 4. lose their roofs 5. electricity

Write About It: Answers will vary.

Focus on Vocabulary — Finish the Paragraphs:
1. coast 2. hurricane 3. rated 4. category 5. natural disaster 6. electricity 7. terrifying 8. nervously 9. damage 10. hillsides

Science Connection — Effects of Hurricanes:
1. 5 2. wind speed 3. category 4. strong buildings 5. category 5

Chasing the Wind **Pages 30–37**

Read and Remember — Choose the Answer:
1. a long, twisted rope 2. took pictures 3. by wind speed 4. in Tornado Alley 5. a mile 6. 20 yards

Think About It — Find the Main Ideas: 2, 3

Focus on Vocabulary — Crossword Puzzle:
ACROSS — 3. thunderstorm 5. chasers 6. destroy 8. scientists 9. accurate
DOWN — 1. tornadoes 2. accident 3. twisters 4. scale 7. spiral

Science Connection — How a Tornado Begins:
1. thundercloud 2. warm air 3. funnel 4. path 5. It draws in more air.

September Surprise **Pages 38–45**

Read and Remember — Check the Events:
2, 4, 6

Write About It: Answers will vary.

Focus on Vocabulary — Finish Up: 1. eye 2. survived 3. shocked 4. shattered 5. elements 6. force 7. huddled 8. pried 9. shambles 10. gushed

Science Connection — A Look at a Hurricane:
1. eye 2. warm air 3. warm ocean water 4. rain 5. no 6. no

Sandstorm! **Pages 46–53**

Read and Remember — Finish the Sentence:
1. Egypt 2. spring 3. donkey 4. flying glass 5. twenty minutes

Think About It — Fact or Opinion: 1. O 2. F 3. O 4. O 5. F 6. F

Focus on Vocabulary — Find the Meaning:
1. dry land that gets little rain 2. storms of blowing sand 3. 2,000 pounds 4. distance something can be seen 5. something that bothers people 6. gave signs of doing harm 7. tied down 8. bits of broken things 9. raised porch 10. pulled up

Science Connection — Sand Dunes: 1. a hill of sand 2. the top 3. a slant 4. the wind 5. a steep slope

Tornado Rips Through Texas Town

Pages 54–61

Read and Remember — Choose the Answer:
1. the Moehrings' house 2. F-5 3. in the bathtub
4. all his cows 5. It was destroyed.

Write About It: Answers will vary.

Focus on Vocabulary — Make a Word:
1. mobile 2. rotating 3. siren 4. amazingly
5. veered 6. horizon 7. survivors 8. foundation
9. mass 10. disaster. The letters in the circles
spell *large house.*

Science Connection — Comparing Tornadoes:
1. The Fujita scale is a chart used to compare
the strengths of tornadoes. 2. 113–157 miles per
hour 3. F-3 4. F-4 5. It pushes cars off the road
and turns over light homes. 6. F-5

Trouble in the Sky Pages 62–69

Read and Remember — Check the Events:
3, 4, 6

Think About It — Drawing Conclusions:
Answers will vary. Here are some possible
conclusions. 1. It was a long flight, and they
grew tired of sitting. 2. They had no warning
something like that was going to happen.
3. They were hurt and they needed medical
attention. 4. Her head was sore because she
had hit it so hard on the ceiling of the plane.

Focus on Vocabulary — Match Up: 1. tools
used to fly a plane 2. sudden bursts of wind
3. height above sea level 4. air that circles the
earth 5. air moving upward 6. air moving
downward 7. a fall through space 8. stopped
going up and down 9. not awake 10. harm to
the body

Science Connection — How an Airplane Flies:
1. nose 2. rudder 3. go up or down 4. wings 5. tail

Killer Wind from the Sea Pages 70–77

Read and Remember — Finish the Sentence:
1. tiring 2. storm 3. strong wind 4. in the salt
mines 5. washed away

Write About It: Answers will vary.

Focus on Vocabulary — Finish the Paragraphs:
1. front 2. developed 3. cyclone 4. salt mines

5. protect 6. evaporate 7. pure 8. directly
9. scrambled 10. disappeared

Science Connection — Storm Names: 1. 4
2. red 3. willy-willy 4. Indian Ocean 5. typhoon

Sammy Sosa Helps Out Pages 78–85

Read and Remember — Choose the Answer:
1. Dominican Republic 2. strong winds 3. a
home-run battle 4. food and medicine 5. It
changed course.

Think About It — Find the Sequence: 1. 4 2. 2
3. 1 4. 5 5. 3

Focus on Vocabulary — Crossword Puzzle:
ACROSS — 4. velocity 5. relief 7. meteorologists
9. dedicated 10. purify DOWN — 1. hometown
2. nation 3. slump 6. course 8. supplies

Science Connection — Weather Map:
1. ⊙ 2. dark green 3. snowy 4. Dallas
5. Miami

A Deadly Day in South Africa

Pages 86–93

Read and Remember — Check the Events:
2, 4, 5

Write About It: Answers will vary.

Focus on Vocabulary — Make a Word:
1. shield 2. lightning 3. bodyguards
4. treatment 5. turmoil 6. zone 7. hail
8. pharmacy 9. vibrating 10. collapse. The
letters in the circles spell *Stan Mzimba.*

Science Connection — How Wind Is Made:
1. cold air 2. cold air 3. Cold air pushes warm
air up. 4. wind 5. It starts to cool.

Blown Away! Pages 94–101

Read and Remember — Finish the Sentence:
1. daughter 2. mother 3. chicken wire 4. in his
car 5. walking down the road

Think About It — Find the Main Ideas: 1, 4

Focus on Vocabulary — Finish Up: 1. recover
2. deputy sheriff 3. confused 4. tree line
5. rubble 6. slight 7. lung 8. overjoyed
9. staggering 10. pinpoint

Science Connection — Tornado Numbers:
1. Oklahoma, Texas, Kansas, Nebraska 2. 52
3. Texas 4. Kansas 5. Nebraska